THE MAGIC OF

Paper Sculpture

THE MAGIC OF
Paper
Sculpture

DAVID SWINTON

CASSELL

A CASSELL BOOK

First published in 1995
by Cassell
Wellington House
125 Strand
London WC2R 0BB

First paperback edition 1997

Designed by The Design Revolution
Illustrations by David and Harry Swinton

Distributed in the United States
by Sterling Publishing Co., Inc.
387 Park Avenue South
New York
New York 10016-8810

British Library Cataloguing-in-Publication data
A catalogue record for this book is available from the British Library.

ISBN 0-304-34887-2

Typeset by Design Revolution
Printed & bound in Slovenia by Printing House DELO-Tiskarna
by arrangement with Korotan Ljubljana

Contents

TO MY FATHER AND MOTHER

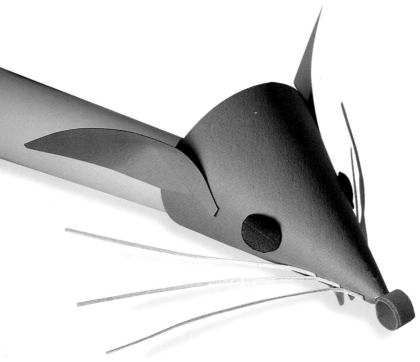

Acknowledgements

I would like to thank all those who have helped with the preparation of this book; the teachers and children who have tried and tested the projects, the many organizations who have provided workshop time and helped me to try such a variety of work, and especially – Harry and Gay Swinton, Tricia Osborne, Hazel Fowler, Julie Collins and Christopher Horridge, Samantha Gray, Ed Barber and John Foster.

The publishers would also like to thank Cowling Wilcox Ltd, for supplying the materials and equipment featured in this book.

Foreword

My first introduction to paper sculpture was when, as a child of about seven years old, against the usual rule, I was allowed to stay up beyond my bedtime and watch my father create bas-relief and three dimensional sculptures on the dining room table.

He was a display artist then and much influenced by Arthur Sadler's *Paper Sculpture*.

On these special occasions, watching the flowing paper forms take shape, as if by magic, the only rule was that I must remain absolutely silent. This was, of course, for my father's benefit, so that he could concentrate on his work and not have to endure constant questions from a very curious and normally talkative little boy. Unknowingly my parents helped me to learn what is probably one of the greatest things I have ever learnt from life.

As I watched in a silence broken only by the sounds of paper, knife, pencil and scissors, I became wrapt in a special sort of concentration. Somehow I saw, and later on was able to recall in tremendous detail, every nuance of the way the tools were used and exactly where and how my father held the paper as he cut it. There was no sense of time passing as I looked on, fascinated, and when my mother did coax me to bed eventually, I could hardly believe it was so late.

Sitting still, keeping quiet and concentrating had seemed no effort at all, so different to my performance in school! Of course, I now know that I had unwittingly discovered how to access the right side of my brain, an essential requirement for artists and all creative people. More of this in the chapter on Paper Sculpture in Education.

The appeal of paper sculpture is that it can transport anyone into the same delights of creativity and spatial awareness as I experienced, all those years ago, with the minimum of time, and of materials and equipment.

At its most basic, any scissors, pencil, paper and glue will do and, unlike origami, in which every fold must be remembered to complete a model, or papier mâché, in which the drying time often outlasts the patience, the art of paper sculpture embodies a simplicity of approach. There are only five basic techniques to learn, very little mess – paper is dry, clean and easily cleared up – and you can achieve spectacular results in both bas-relief and three dimensions. Unlike many artistic disciplines, you will find that you need not be especially gifted or able to draw in order to create perfect paper sculptures – all that is required to give you the satisfaction of creating your own sculptures is a little time and determination.

MAKING A START

The projects in this book are arranged loosely in order of complexity and start with paper sculptures that demonstrate the basic techniques followed by more ambitious pieces. The technical section contains all the hints and tips I have learned from over forty years' experience with paper sculpture and I know that some of the information, even on simple things like cutting and folding, will be new to you.

Please study the five basic techniques – CUT, FOLD, CURL, BEND, SCORE – because the instructions in each project assume you are familiar with all five, and similarly with GLUING.

I have planned the book so that those of you who wish to read and contemplate before you act may do so and those of a different disposition, possibly with some experience of paper sculpture already, can get straight into the action.

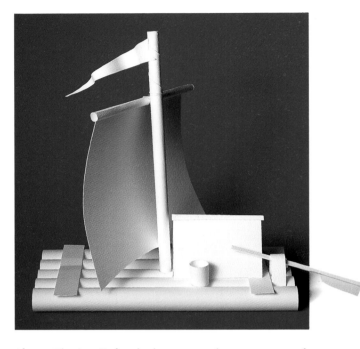

Above: The Log Raft is built on a simple construction of cylinders.

Below: These paper waves conjure up a vision of a choppy sea – ideal for the galleon on pages 92–95.

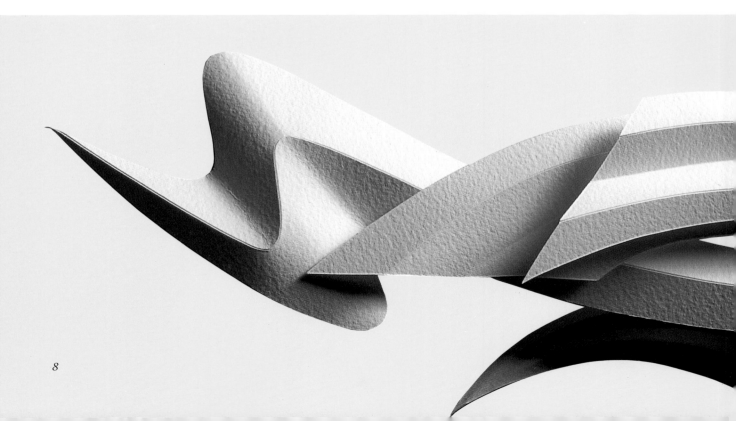

All the projects have accompanying diagrams to support and illuminate the text. The saying 'a picture is worth a thousand words' is very true here and, to make doubly sure of successful results, I have provided a set of templates which are drawn to scale, suitable for enlarging on a photocopier.

Photographs of the finished pieces will also repay careful study.

There are sixteen projects in the book, covering a wide variety of subjects. All have been tried and tested by the thousands of junior school children, ranging in age from eight to thirteen years, who have attended my workshops. It is so much easier to learn things when you are young and I have enjoyed teaching simple paper sculptures such as the *Lantern* and *Letterbox, Leaves* and *Flowers* to children as young as five.

Paper is traditionally described by artists in terms of portrait and landscape, depending on which way round it is placed in relation to the viewer. I have always found this terminology a nuisance when conducting workshops, as the words do not give a clear enough clue as to which way round the paper should be. Linking word and image proves to be more successful and I now call these positions FLATS (portrait) and HOUSES (landscape). A vertical sheet looks like a block of flats and an imaginary roof will convert a horizontal piece of paper into a house. To avoid confusion, I have added the portrait and landscape conventions in brackets throughout the book.

Historically many cultures including China, Poland, Mexico, France and England, have produced cut paper motifs and these prepared the way for the development of modern paper sculpture. This originated in Poland as classroom exercises in three dimensional design, devised by Professor Wojciech Jastrzebowski, (1884–1963), at a private art school for young women in Cracow. The success of these initial forays into working with paper encouraged him to continue teaching paper sculpture to his students at the Academy of Fine Arts in Warsaw from 1923 onwards.

Above: Paper is available in a range of colours.

Tadeusz Lipski, a graduate of the Warsaw Academy, had a one-man exhibition in London popularizing the art during the last war, and his work was soon being commissioned by exhibition designers in Britain. Arthur Sadler, already mentioned, and Bruce Angrave were two English pioneers.

Much in vogue during the 1950s for window and exhibition display, and since used almost exclusively for commercial art purposes, paper sculpture has rarely, if ever, been used as a serious sculptural medium in the fine art field.

Chinese tradition says that paper was invented by Tsai Lun in AD 105, since when it has become an indispensible part of all our lives. Despite predictions that the computer age would reduce our paper needs, we now use more paper than ever before and, unlike past ages in which paper was valued as a precious resource, we now experience paper mostly as a commonplace, disposable material, manufactured in any number of different colours and finishes for as many different uses. Following is a useful chart for paper conversions.

I hope this book will help you appreciate some of the special qualities inherent in paper when used as a sculptural medium, and perhaps inspire a paper sculptor of the future.

If, however, your aims are more modest and, like myself, you simply enjoy making things, then get your scissors, paper, pencil and glue ready, and we'll make a start.

PAPER SIZES		
AO	841 x 1189 mm	33 $1/8$ x 46 $3/4$ inches
A1	594 x 841 mm	23 $3/8$ x 33 $1/8$ inches
A2	420 x 594 mm	16 $1/2$ x 23 $3/8$ inches
A3	297 x 420 mm	11 $3/4$ x 16 $1/2$ inches
A4	210 x 297 mm	8 $1/4$ x 11 $3/4$ inches
A5	148 x 210 mm	5 $7/8$ x 8 $1/4$ inches
A6	104 x 149 mm	4 $1/5$ x 6 inches

Right: Paper sculpture figures by the author.

EQUIPMENT AND MATERIALS

Superb paper sculptures can be created with the simplest of equipment and materials. Confident cutting with a good pair of scissors or a sharp craft knife, using tabs and slits to join the paper, results in lively, original work. But to enjoy this kind of freedom requires much experience and most of us will need a few basic items of equipment in order to obtain excellent results in this art.

Nearly all households and certainly all schools will have some of the equipment and materials discussed below. Some equipment is absolutely essential to the projects in this book, and there are also some luxury items which can make jobs easier or quicker. However, in general, the range of items you need to get started is minimal.

OPTIONAL EQUIPMENT

LARGE CRAFT KNIFE

SET SQUARE

'T' SQUARE

TAPE MEASURE

PAPER PUNCH (multi-head)

STAPLER • GUN TACKER

HOUSEHOLD PAINT BRUSH (small)

ELECTRIC JIGSAW

HOT GLUE GUN

GENERAL WOODWORKING EQUIPMENT
for making armatures

BASIC EQUIPMENT

SCISSORS

SMALL CRAFT KNIFE or SCALPEL
with straight-edged disposable blades

30 cm (1 ft) PLASTIC RULE

STEEL RULE or METAL STRAIGHT EDGE
(safety type for children)

THICK CARD or CUTTING MAT

2B, HB and 3H PENCILS

COCKTAIL STICKS

COMPASSES

SOFT, WHITE PLASTIC ERASER or
PUTTY RUBBER

TRACING SHEET

SCISSORS

You will need good quality scissors with blades at least 15 cm (6 in) in length, preferably with pointed ends. Larger scissors are even better if you can handle them. My favourite are large dressmakers' shears. Some paper sculptors prefer stainless steel scissors with moulded plastic handles and very sharp blades. A small pair of these is very useful for cutting out details and tiny curves. Small blunt-ended, cheap, poorly rivetted pairs, similar to those found in many schools, are to be avoided at all costs.

SCALPEL

I prefer scalpel handles which take detachable blades so I can discard them as soon as they become blunt. A sharp, straight blade is infinitely preferable to the curved sort. Any small, very sharp, straight-bladed craft knife will suffice. My father patiently sharpens his blades on a tiny oilstone, but I have the modern disease of no time for such luxuries and replace mine as soon as they loose their point or edge.

STEEL RULE

A steel rule helps to guide the scalpel, or craft knife, accurately when cutting and scoring straight lines. Children could use a paper trimmer for cutting large sheets of paper and, when scoring with a knife is necessary, ensure they use a metal safety rule which offers some protection.

TRACING SHEET

A tracing sheet allows you to transfer drawn patterns to your sculpture paper, and is particularly useful when you are using expensive watercolour paper. Make the tracing sheet by scribbling with a soft pencil, 4B or 6B, all over one side of a piece of very thin paper (layout, detail, typing or photocopying paper). I have A4 ($8^1/4$ x $11^3/4$ in) and A3 ($11^3/4$ x $16^1/2$ in) sheets in my studio because I find these the two most useful sizes. Once the paper is covered with graphite, rub it in well with a small pad of soft tissues, which removes excess graphite at the same time. This sheet of homemade graphite paper will last you a long time – I've had mine for fifteen years now – and has the advantage of making a very light grey mark which can be easily removed with a putty rubber.

To use the tracing sheet, sandwich it graphite side down between the drawing to be transferred on top and your chosen paper beneath. Use a sharp 3H pencil to go over the drawing or pattern lines to trace the image. A few small scraps of masking tape will prevent the sheets moving, especially if you are transferring a complicated image. Don't press too hard with your pencil or you will groove the paper, but check that your traced drawing is appearing after you have gone over a few lines. There is nothing more infuriating than, after an hour's work, finding that your graphite sheet is upside down or that you haven't used sufficient pressure and your paper is virtually blank! A tracing sheet will work well with photocopies of the project patterns in this book. Because most of my work is for exhibitions and commissions, I usually trace patterns the wrong way round on the reverse side of my paper to avoid graphite marks.

COCKTAIL STICKS

Cocktail sticks are excellent for applying glues such as PVA as they allow you to spread the glue thinly over the paper surface or accurately down the edge of a cylinder. Far superior to any other glue spreaders for delicate work, the practicality of cocktail sticks is a tip supplied by my mother who uses them for sticking down tiny petals in dried flower pictures. Children soon master the art of using them and create less mess and waste less glue as a result. When using cocktail sticks use a shallow glue container, such as a saucer.

MISCELLANEOUS ITEMS

Plastic glue spreaders and small house painting brushes are best used to cover larger areas of paper with PVA.

A strong pair of compasses and a couple of erasers – a soft, white plastic one and a putty rubber – will complete your range of basic equipment.

OPTIONAL EXTRAS

On the luxury list the most useful pieces of equipment are a heavy duty craft knife for cutting card, an office stapler and a tape measure. If you are planning to do large work for exhibitions and displays, a gun tacker and a hot glue gun are a worthwhile investment, and an electric jigsaw enables you to cut out armatures quickly from sheet materials.

BASIC MATERIALS

PAPER

cartridge, 135gsm

3-sheet pulp board, 230 microns

*watercolour paper (HP, NOT and
ROUGH surfaces)*

coloured papers, 135gsm or 230 microns

thin typing paper or photocopying paper

CARD

greyboard • white card

corrugated card (boxes)

TRACING PAPER

ROUGH PAPER for patterns and sketches

PVA GLUE • CLEAR ADHESIVE TAPE

MASKING TAPE

ADDITIONAL MATERIALS

DOUBLE-SIDED TAPE

PVA GLUE

ADHESIVE FOAM PADS

*CLEAR SOLVENT-BASED ADHESIVE
(please note health warning)*

MOULDABLE ADHESIVE

*N.B. Various other items may be mentioned
in the text principally in the section on
DISPLAY and EXHIBITION.*

PAPER

Paper is the most important material and, while many different papers may be used for sculptures, I describe here a few that are useful for most work and that I have tried and tested myself in my professional work and in workshops.

PULP BOARD & CARTRIDGE

Three-sheet pulp board is the paper I use most. It is really a thin printer's board but has just the right strength, springiness and resilience for paper sculpture. It is available in all the sizes up to A1 ($23^3/8$ x $33^1/8$ in) and is not costly. Pulp board of 230 microns thickness is excellent for small work and thicker grades are available for larger sculptures. Cartridge paper (135 gsm) is a superior alternative which has a slight tooth or texture to its surface and, again, is available in all sizes up to A1 ($23^3/8$ x $33^1/8$ in).

WATERCOLOUR PAPER

For exhibition work I mostly use a NOT surface watercolour paper. This can be wood-pulp or cotton-based, the latter being more durable. Watercolour paper is made in three surface finishes – HP (hot-pressed) which is smooth; NOT (not hot-pressed) which has a medium texture and ROUGH, which has a pronounced texture excellent for large sculptures where its roughness adds interest to the otherwise plain paper surface. The one disadvantage of a rough surface is that it soon collects dust.

Watercolour papers are inevitably more expensive but worth the investment for their superior handling properties and quality surface. The thickness of watercolour papers is usually shown by giving the weight of a ream of five hundred sheets, from 90lbs, the thinnest, to 300lbs, the thickest.

Handmade watercolour paper will both curl and roll well in each direction because the fibres in the sheets are distributed in a more random pattern than any of the machine-made papers. These have a grain that runs in one direction only, and are more easily curled or rolled in the direction of the grain. Gently flex machine-made paper to see which way it curves more naturally. Try and make all your cylinders, curls and folds in the direction of the grain.

COLOURED PAPER

Coloured papers, particularly bright shades, are more expensive than the white variety, but offer a wide range of different effects to the paper sculptor. Coloured cartridge and pulp boards are available in the same sizes and weights as their white equivalents. Your local paper mill should be able to supply these in bulk and a printer may sell you smaller quantities. Tinted watercolour papers can be bought in most art materials shops or through Educational Supplier's catalogues.

THIN PAPERS

Thin typing or photocopying paper is used for making slim rolls. However, check that its whiteness matches your main sculpture paper, which can vary from brilliant white to slightly beige, cream or even a greyish tint.

WHITE & COLOURED CARD

White and coloured card can be allowed to show as part of the sculpture, provided it matches the shade or colour of the paper you are using. In fact, if you have access to a supplier of pulp board, you can order thicker grades to match exactly your basic paper. Self-coloured card is especially useful to make larger versions of many of the sculptures in this book.

GREYBOARD

Greyboard, useful for backing work and for interior structural supports for larger sculptures, can be purchased in single sheets up to A1 (23³/8 x 33¹/8 in) or in bundles, sold by weight.

CORRUGATED CARD

I go to the supermarket to replenish my store of corrugated cardboard boxes. I also have a large roll of the sort used for packing, which is smooth on one side only. Both are ideal for spacing material (see Spacing Paper, pp.25–27).

If in doubt about a paper's suitability for paper sculpture, try using it for all five basic techniques – cut, fold, curl, bend and score – and if it survives these it should be alright. Of course, large work demands heavier paper.

TRACING PAPER

Tracing paper is excellent if you need repeats of a complicated shape. Trace your original then turn the tracing paper over and burnish the image on to the back of your sculpture paper with the

handle of a smooth teaspoon. If you use a soft 2B pencil for the tracing, this method will allow several burnishings. The image can then be cut from the back, keeping the front surface pristine. This process works just as well the correct way round but you will need to remove the graphite marks with a putty rubber.

ADHESIVES

PVA is a water-based, white plastic glue which dries waterproof and colourless. It is a strong, all-purpose adhesive and can be used confidently for paper sculpture work. It takes a short time to dry if applied correctly but will stay tacky long enough to allow some adjustment of pieces. In addition, it is excellent for miniature work when it can be applied with the end of a pin. If you accidentally get some on your clothes, remove it immediately with cold water and, similarly, wash out brushes before they dry.

Clear solvent-based adhesive is unsuitable for children. It should be used only in a well-ventilated room (see health warning on label). Its advantages are that it is quick drying, has a slight elasticity and will not cockle even thin papers. I use it mainly for large exhibition work. Unlike PVA it has a tendency to string when applied and this can be awkward when gluing small items.

ADHESIVE TAPES

Masking tape is good for the temporary fixing of roughs and models and can also be used for holding pieces while glue dries. However, take care that it does not damage your paper surface. Masking tape, clear adhesive tape, double-sided tape and adhesive foam pads all have their uses.

PLASTERS

Keep a box of plasters handy. Blood is impossible to remove without damaging the paper surface.

As with all arts and crafts, buy the best materials and equipment you can afford and you will be able to get on with the creative side of the work with confidence.

FIVE BASIC TECHNIQUES

TECHNIQUES – CUT

Keep your scissor blades open as you cut sheets of paper for all the projects in this book. Holding them wide apart gives more control when cutting, particularly around curves. Many people learn to snip the blades shut each time they make a cut but this is to be avoided at all costs because it can take small nicks out of the paper, giving a jagged edge to the work.

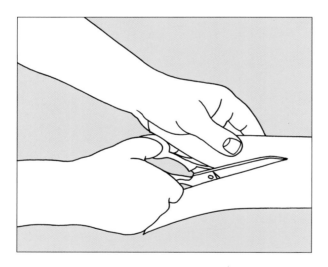

Information on the most suitable scissors for paper sculpture is given in the previous chapter, *Equipment and Materials*, so I only need to repeat here that sharp, pointed scissors, of a reasonable length, are ideal for all normal requirements. Left-handers generally benefit from using scissors designed specially for them.

Small pieces of paper can be cut while seated but you will need to stand or kneel to cut larger sheets, resting the free end of the paper on the table top or floor. Younger children and those with disabilities often find it difficult to cut the whole way across a large sheet, in which case it is best to let them cut halfway and then turn the paper round and start at the opposite side to meet the first cut in the middle. Most people can manage to cut neatly halfway through a large piece of paper and it is only then that the sheet tends to flop about and obstruct the cutting process, creating wobbly edges.

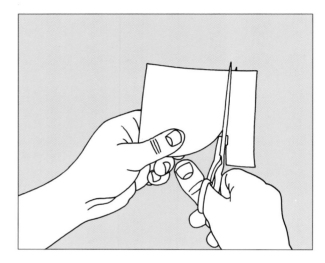

When you start, hold the paper near to where you are cutting, thumb on top, to control the edge and keep it still. Hold small rectangular pieces of paper by the vertical side opposite the side you are cutting. Be careful not to damage your paper by holding it too tightly, especially if it is thin. Unintentional creases can easily mar the surface of a finished sculpture.

While cutting curves, try and turn the paper (clockwise for right-handers and anti-clockwise for left-handers) rather than the scissors, and adopt a much smaller cutting stroke. The tighter the curve the smaller these strokes need to be – almost a nervous twitch of the fingers on the scissors when cutting circles. Children in particular will find this method a real boon because it will enable them to cut complicated curvilinear shapes with accuracy and confidence.

I use a scalpel or small craft knife for cutting most of my own work as this gives a cleaner edge than scissors, particularly with thicker papers and thin card. Use a metal rule (the safety type is preferable for children) to guide the scalpel for

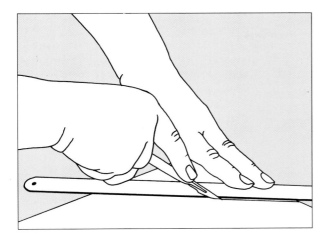

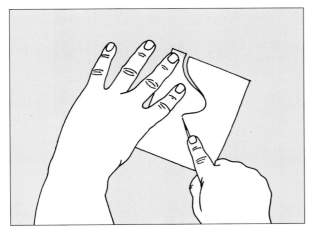

straight cuts. Try to move the paper for freehand cutting, rather than the knife, always keeping the other hand well clear of the blade.

Use a stout card base to protect your worksurface when you cut with a knife or scalpel. Hold the scalpel at a low angle, with the blade upright, extending your forefinger to guide the cutting edge. Keep your hand on top of the handle in the same way that you would hold a dinner knife, rather than how you would hold a pencil. Alternatives to the cardboard base are a sheet of plate glass or a special laminated plastic, self-healing cutting mat. The skill of making neat cuts in paper will allow you to make this stunning Lantern (see pages 42–44).

Right: Crisp cutting on a decorative lantern.

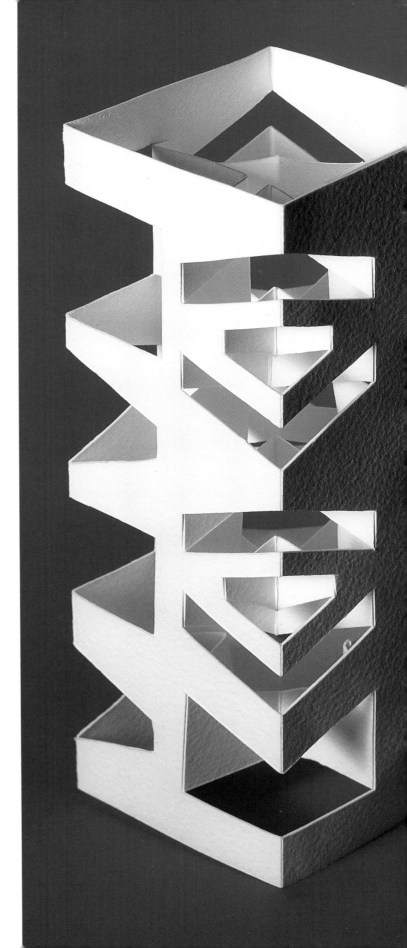

TECHNIQUES – FOLD

'There's more than one way of killing a pig', is a saying of my father's which often comes to mind when I am wrestling with a practical problem which is difficult to solve, and looking for alternative ways to do so. There are several problems inherent in the folding process which can make it difficult to accomplish perfectly.

We are all likely to cut and fold paper in the same way as the person who taught us originally, perhaps with a few minor modifications in technique as we get older. This is why most people match the corners with one hand then crease the paper with the other. However, this method rarely gives good results because the paper is too free to move. Some try to avoid this problem by matching both sets of corners and then find they either need to grow a third hand to do the creasing, or compromise by awkwardly using their knee or chin!

I used to fold in a similar way until I started to teach paper sculpture professionally and needed to evolve a method which was more reliable and successful. Large sheets are always more awkward to manage than small ones, however, I would advise standing at a table or kneeling on the floor, while you learn the following technique, whatever the size of your paper.

The first important principle is always to fold the sheet away from yourself. If you are right-handed then put your left hand gently on top to support and steady the paper once it has been curved over. Avoid pressing down, or making any creases or dents in the edge to be folded, at this stage. Slip your right hand in between the two sides, resting it on the bottom half and holding the top sheet in place with your right thumb.

Slide your left hand forwards, near to the edge of the top half of the sheet and use both hands to adjust the two edges and match the corners. Be sure to keep your hands in these positions and do not be tempted to move them to the corners.

Once the two sides match perfectly, press down firmly with the left hand to prevent any movement of the paper. Let go of the edge with your right hand and turn it palm upwards, placing your fingers against the heel of the left hand. Move your right hand back towards you to fold the centre of the paper, then move it briskly right and left to complete the task.

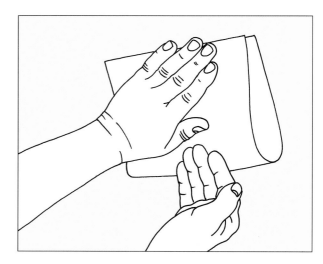

As soon as you are practised in this technique, you will find you can fold large sheets very accurately. Small pieces need a slight variation in that only the fingers of each hand are used to hold and fold. Left-handers who, it is said, are much more creative than the rest of us, please reverse all the above instructions.

Once the paper has been folded, it will need creasing. Use the fingernails or a rule to do this, pressing firmly from the centre to the edge of your paper in both directions.

If you want to cut along a foldline, reverse fold the paper and crease it again to make the paper

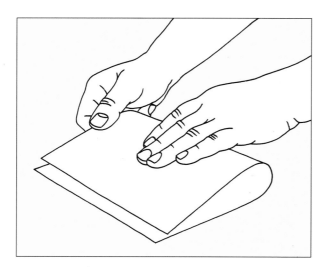

lie flat, once it is opened out, ready for you to wield your scissors. Cut without the extra folding and creasing and your scissors will tend to wander from side to side, giving a wavy edge to both sheets of paper.

When folding a thin edge, you must change

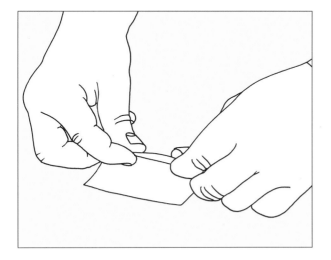

your technique completely and keep all your fingers on top of the sheet with your thumbs underneath; both hands should be at right angles to the fold. Again folding away from yourself, bend over the desired width of paper until your thumbs are on top and together near the centre. Slide both thumbs outwards, guiding the paper between thumbs and fingers, creasing as you go. With fanfolding, this technique is repeated until the paper is concertinaed from end to end. At this stage press all the folds together and crease them again, with fingers or rule, to ensure a crisp finish to your work.

'It's difficult to teach an old dog new tricks', is my father's cry when he wants to avoid doing the housework now he is retired. I do understand that you may fold in a completely different way to me so, when trying this method for the first time, you may find the manipulations strange and feel like using my father's excuse. Please persevere until it becomes familiar and ceases to be a new trick, and you will find you can fold any size of paper confidently and with accuracy.

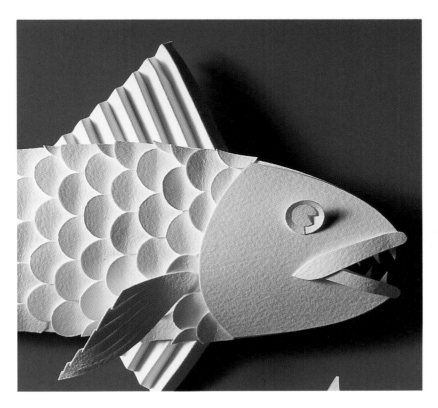

Left: The fish's fin has been concertina folded.

TECHNIQUES – CURL

I have probably mentioned the curling technique and all those words associated with it – curling, curled, curly, curved – more than any other in this book. This is because curling is such an essential, easy and indispensible way of giving life to a flat piece of paper.

All paper is made of fibres, the most common being wood and cotton. When paper is curled, the fibres on the inside are squashed together while those on the outside are stretched. With very thick paper you can sometimes see this effect, with cracks appearing on the outside and ridges on the inner surface of the sheet. This gives us our first rule of thumb: the thinner the paper, the easier it is to curl.

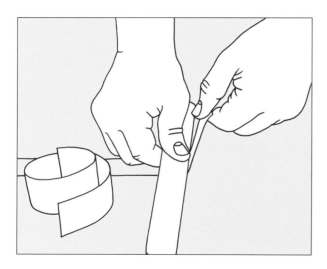

Paper can be curled by drawing it from under a rule but I am happier using the closed blades of a pair of scissors to do the same job. Hold the scissors upside down in whichever hand you use, thumb on top of the paper to guide it over the closed blades. The secret of successful curling is to turn the hand holding the scissors outwards before pulling the closed blades gently and steadily along the paper.

Most people prefer to move the scissor hand, but pulling the paper strip is just as successful provided you have the opposite wrist well turned. Be careful not to hold your thumb down too firmly, or pull hard, as you may tear off the curl. For young children, a hexagonal pencil may be substituted for scissors and works reasonably well but, again, success depends on turning the pulling hand outwards once the paper strip is secured under the thumb.

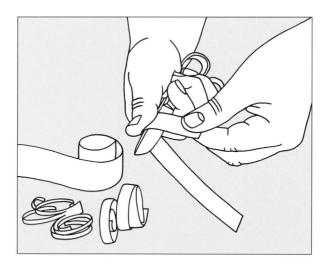

Those who have difficulty mastering this technique can make excellent curls by rolling the paper tightly around a suitable former, such as a round pencil, dowel or strong cardboard roll. This method is inevitably slower and it is worth persevering with scissors so that both skills can be used where necessary. Both scissor and pencil techniques are more suitable for curling small pieces of paper, thin strips or details on sculptures than larger sheets.

When you need to curl larger sheets into cylinders, pull the paper over the sharp edge of a table or worktop. A rounded edge to the table will not achieve the correct result. Press firmly with the left hand, keeping it flat on the paper, and pull with the finger and thumb of the right hand. Move your upper hand as your other hand pulls the paper over the edge of the table downwards, towards the floor. Turn the paper round, being careful to place it the same way up, and curl the other end, then roll it up with both hands to create a loose cylinder.

I always kneel on the floor, next to the worktop, facing right, when demonstrating this technique to children. When they kneel it is easier for them to pull the paper towards the floor, which gives the best curl and thereby makes the paper much easier for them to work with. Bear in mind successful results will encourage them in the craft. Left-handers must face the other way round and, as usual, swap hands!

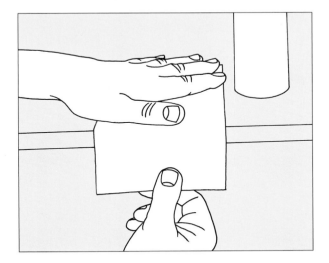

Take care not to crease your paper when curling large sheets – pull the edge carefully and steadily, keeping the upper hand parallel to the edge of the table. With smaller pieces, the upper hand needs to be at right angles to the sheet.

Curling thin widths can be very awkward because there is precious little paper to hold and pull. A much easier option is to curl a longer piece and then cut off the desired width once the paper has been relaxed and stretched. A pencil or dowel will help you to roll it into a cylinder and can also be used to hold the glued overlap in position while the adhesive dries.

If you cannot avoid curling thin widths, curl in the direction of the grain and use all your fingers together, as if you were playing a piano, to pull the paper over a sharp table edge.

Practise making small cylinders with rough paper until you become adept at the skill, always joining the two edges by gluing the overlapping one. This overlap will be 1 cm (½ in) for small cylinders and will seldom need to be more than about 4 cm (1½ in) even for the largest cylinder made from standard sheets of paper or card.

Right: All the hair was curled for this paper portrait.

TECHNIQUES – BEND

Bending divides into two similar ways of shaping the paper: pulling it into a soft, angled fold or gently stroking the paper to curve it, between fingers and thumb.

The former is used to change the direction of the paper more acutely than curling but less acutely than folding. Bend it as you would a piece of wire, except that paper may need to be bent several times before it will hold its position. A change in direction may be given before construction or when a part is in situ.

The latter technique is similar to curling with scissors in that the hand doing the bending must turn over as it pulls the paper. Hold the paper in both your hands, fingers upwards, thumbs underneath, and stroke it, turning the wrist of the moving hand as you go to make the strip or piece pass over the thumb. This pull must be directly opposite the holding hand or you may tear the paper. Done correctly with the thumb and fingers you will achieve a gentle curve. Scissors and rule are not so sensitive as the fingers and tend to stretch and curl a piece.

Using this method with care, you may be able to bend small pieces of paper attached to a sculpture if they look too flat. In this instance, the stroking movement can only be done with one

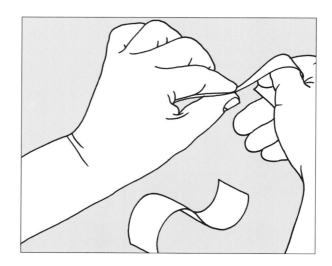

hand because the other is needed to hold the sculpture still.

Bending can also be used to relax strips of thicker paper prior to curling and helps to prevent unsightly stretch marks on the surface.

Keep your hands spotlessly clean while handling the paper in this way to minimize finger marks. In hot weather keep your hands dry by dusting them with French chalk or talcum powder or, if you prefer, you can wear a pair of thin, white cotton gloves.

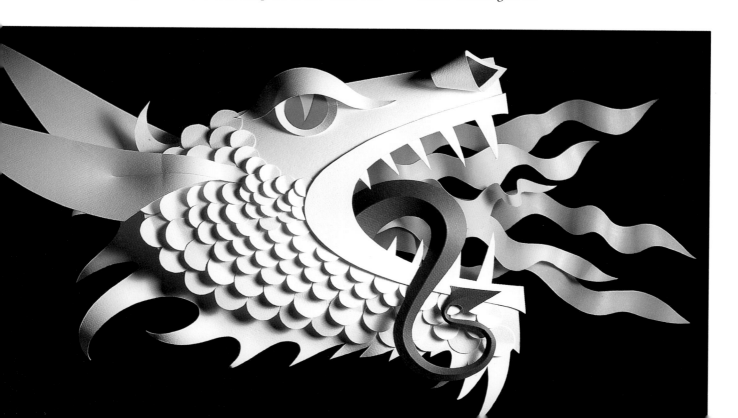

TECHNIQUES – SCORE

Scoring is, like curling, one of the main techniques for shaping paper sculpture and usually makes a major contribution to the typically sharp, clean, lines of a finished work.

Scoring is usually done with a small, sharp craft knife or scalpel, pressing just hard enough to cut part-way through the paper surface. Remember to protect your workbench or table with a cutting mat, such as a sheet of thick card, in case you press too hard and sever the paper completely.

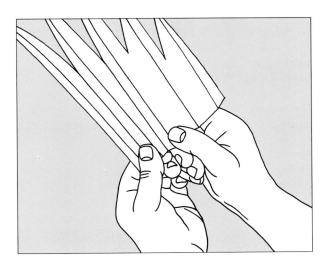

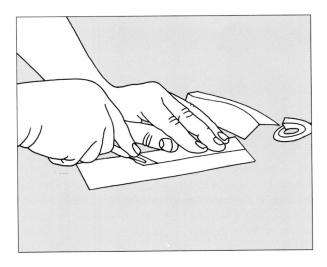

Clear adhesive tape will repair minor accidents of this sort when applied to the reverse of the scoreline but do try to avoid cutting through.

Always bend the paper back from the scoreline to crease it, because this is the only way to obtain the correct, sharp edge so typical of this technique. The sharp edge distinguishes scoring from folding. In addition, scoring enables you to produce angled and curved shapes with ease.

Scoring and creasing reduces the width of the paper by approximately half, parallel to the scoreline, depending on the depth of the corrugation. When scoring alternate sides, with wing feathers for example, crease the first set of lines to give accurate positioning for the completion of the scored work on the reverse side of your paper.

Left: The dragon's flames show the effectiveness of the bending technique.

Score and crease tapered shapes starting at the wide end and moving towards the narrow end or point. Creasing circles and curves reduces their diameter, so pull them carefully inwards with your fingers as you make the crease.

Younger children of four to six years old will find a compass point, dividers or even an empty ballpoint pen pressed down firmly, can be used to score paper with reasonable success. If you do use a craft knife, make sure you keep your free hand well away from the blade, preferably behind it.

Knives or other scoring instruments need to be held at a shallow angle to the paper. Hold them as described in the section on CUTTING (see p.16). This allows a smoother scoreline to be drawn with greater control and avoids scratching up the paper surface. There is also less chance of accidentally cutting yourself when you handle the knife or scalpel correctly. I keep plasters handy near my workbench as a precaution.

Use a metal safety rule for straight scoring, holding the knife at a shallow angle, forefinger forward, to guide the blade. When free scoring, move the paper while keeping the knife steady.

Having been a teacher, I am very much aware of the risks inherent in allowing children to use very sharp tools. I teach youngsters of eight years and upwards to use them correctly and then supervise any scoring by having only one knife and cutting mat, which are on my desk. If in any doubt, you will find a sharp pair of compasses or dividers a satisfactory substitute.

FURTHER TECHNIQUES

GLUING

Your gluing technique needs to be immaculate for paper sculpture. Glue must not end up on the finished, outer surface of the paper. To achieve the control necessary for spreading glue efficiently, I advocate using wooden cocktail sticks.

PVA is my recommended adhesive for all home and school use because it is completely non-toxic. A washable PVA is available for the very young who may have a tendency to get it on to their clothes as well as their work! It is a white, water-based glue which dries to a clear, water-proof finish.

A major disadvantage is that it damps the paper, which can cause cockling but, if it is applied correctly with a cocktail stick, the amount of glue can be kept to a minimum and this problem avoided. I prefer not to use glue-spreaders for work with paper because I find it difficult to regulate the amount of adhesive being applied, but these do seem to be alright for cardboard.

Cocktail sticks can be used confidently with paper up to A1 (33$\frac{1}{8}$ x 23$\frac{3}{8}$ in) size. Not only are they excellent for spreading glue along a join but their fine points even allow accurate, controlled application of adhesive along the thin edges of paper pieces.

Use saucers or similar shallow containers with cocktail sticks and PVA because they are apt to cause less mess than a deep pot as it is easier to judge the amount of glue you are picking up. A squeezy bottle of PVA for topping up the saucers periodically will make the gluing process even more economical.

Applying the glue is best done with your sheet of paper laid level with the edge of the table and the cocktail stick held at right angles to this edge.

Place a blob of glue at the top and push it quickly along the edge, spreading the glue thinly and replenishing this with the cocktail stick where necessary.

Where there are two pieces of paper or two edges to be joined spread glue on the underside of the overlapping one, if possible, to avoid excess adhesive and sticky finger marks along the join. Although this seems a logical choice, it is surprising how many people spread glue on the wrong side of the paper.

A stiff brush (artist's oil brush or house-painting type) or a plastic spreader is useful for gluing larger areas and is essential for cardboard, which can be very absorbent and may need a generous amount of PVA before it will stick together. For very large sheets of paper you will still need to spread the glue as thinly as you can.

In the case of accidental spillage remove PVA as soon as possible, before it has a chance to dry, with a cloth and plenty of cold water. Once dry, normal PVA is waterproof, although the washable variety can still be removed from clothes, furniture and carpets with cold water.

As I have already mentioned in the chapter on Equipment and Materials, I use clear solvent-based adhesive for all my exhibition work because it is very strong, transparent and quick-drying glue, and will not cockle even the thinnest of papers. It is not suitable for school use because of its solvent base but, if you do decide to use it at home, please observe the health warning printed on the packet and work in a well-ventilated room. Manufacturers will advise on cleaning it from clothing and other materials.

The advantage of both PVA and clear solvent-based adhesive is that they dry to a clear finish so that the effect of any adhesive finding its way to the outer surface of your paper sculpture is much minimalized.

If PVA is not available to you, any glue will do provided it gives you the results you want and is used with care. In the past I have used rubber-based glue, flour paste, wallpaper paste, brown and white wood glue, rubber cement, balsa cement and so on to create my paper sculptures. Don't allow the lack of a particular glue at any given time to hamper your creative urges – use whatever glue you have to hand.

MARKING PAPER

Marks of any kind, especially pencil marks, are anathema to paper sculpture and will spoil the pristine surface needed for this art, particularly when white paper is used. This is one of the reasons I have kept the drawing required in the project section of the book to a minimum and, in some cases, encouraged you to cut direct with scissors or a craft knife. This is a very exciting approach to the art of paper sculpture, particularly for children and also adults who can find drawing rather an inhibiting activity. Direct cutting also taps straight into the creativity of the right side of the brain.

GRAPHITE MARKS

I avoid the problem of marks by always drawing and tracing my sculpture in reverse before cutting out, but this method can be awkward for beginners who will prefer to work 'right way round'. This practice does, however, save time in rubbing out traces of pencil and the inevitable damage this causes to the surface of the paper. When you are more experienced, you may prefer to work in this way.

ERASERS & PENCILS

If you do need to use an eraser get a good quality, soft plastic one for harder papers such as cartridge and pulp boards and a putty rubber for handmade and watercolour papers. A putty rubber will even lift pencil successfully from a textured surface because its slightly tacky composition allows you to use a dabbing action to remove the graphite.

If you must draw on the front of the paper, use a sharp 2B pencil, lightly held, as the soft lead is removed more easily. If you scribble on the back of a drawing or use a tracing sheet, as described in the chapter on Materials and Equipment, go over the lines with a sharp 3H pencil, which is much harder and will produce a thin, crisp line. Check that you are pressing just enough to transfer the drawing. When I use either of these last two methods, working 'right way round', I cut just inside the marked line to eliminate any erasing and all pencil marks.

FINGER MARKS

Finger marks are much more difficult to remove and I prefer to avoid these by keeping my hands scrupulously clean. If they perspire in summer, a light dressing of French chalk or scentless talc will help to keep them dry.

GLUE MARKS

If used quickly, a damp, lint-free cotton cloth will remove glue spots and excess PVA, but the slightest over-dampening will cause the paper to cockle. Once glue is dry, the only option may be to scrape it off with the edge of a sharp blade and then burnish the fibres down by rubbing the blemished paper through a cover sheet. This is seldom satisfactory and I always replace the sheet.

There are also several types of proprietary solutions on the market which claim to remove glues and finger marks from paper, but I believe it is easier to make a real effort to work cleanly in the first place. If you do have marks on the front of your sculpture remove all of these, if you can, before you begin shaping or scoring.

SHAPING ALLOWANCE

When working from an original drawing, remember to make allowance in width or length where the paper is to be curved or pleated in either direction. I usually add an extra third when curving pieces and adjust any drawing accordingly. Experience is the best teacher as to how much to add to any shape and you will soon acquire an eye to judge the extra needed. Obviously it is preferable to err on the generous side as paper can always be trimmed, but additions are messy. When using expensive watercolour paper, make a same size model in cartridge paper, which can be easily adjusted beforehand and will ensure all pieces fit. All these patterns can be marked out on the reverse of the watercolour paper.

Allowances for pleating need to be much bigger than for curving. Once scored and creased, paper may be only a third to a quarter of its original size in the direction of the pleating. As a case in point, I have often had to make extra feathers for wings because of underestimating the amount needed for pleats, or fan-folds.

A PERFECT FINISH

Keep your sculptures spotlessly clean by avoiding unnecessary marks, having a very tidy working environment and by adopting a methodical approach to drawing out, constructing and gluing your sculptures. The final effect of your sculpture will only be really successful if the paper is clear of marks such as glue spots or finger prints.

JOINING PAPER

There are always times when your sheet of paper isn't big enough for the job in hand. Some manufacturers make long lengths of paper sold in sizeable rolls but their main disadvantage is that the inherent curl is difficult to remove if you require flat pieces for your sculpture, so I prefer to join several smaller sheets. Butt and overlap joins are two simple ways of doing this.

BUTT-JOINS

Using this technique, two sheets are placed with their edges together and a strip of paper, at least 2.5 cm (1 in) wide, is glued on, overlapping each sheet equally. Great care must be taken to avoid any excess glue squeezing up into the join. I mark the centre of the strip before applying a small amount of glue to it and then attach the first sheet to the left side of the strip. Add the second sheet, pushing gently until the two match exactly. Butt-joining is the most useful technique for sculptures in which only the front of the sheet is showing, the strip being hidden inside or behind the work.

OVERLAP JOINING

In pieces where both sides of the sheet are to be seen, use an overlap join. This overlap needs to be marked faintly and neatly on one sheet and glue applied up to the line before placing the second sheet on top. Make sure this top sheet covers the guide line so you won't need to erase it later. For both sorts of joining, PVA allows a little slip for good positioning before it grips, but it will cockle thin paper because of its water content if applied too liberally.

DOUBLE-SIDED TAPE

Double-sided tape does not allow any slip or re-positioning but it is useful if there is little time for glue to dry as when demonstrating the art of paper sculpture in public. Double-sided tape is more effective when used for thinner papers, such as cartridge or pulp board, even when pieces are under some tension. Watercolour and hand-made papers in thicker grades, and card, are much more secure when glued together. When using double-sided adhesive tape, take care to smooth it down accurately from one end, avoiding wrinkles and overlaps.

Double-sided tape is adhesive on both sides and has a backing which must be peeled off once one side is stuck down. Burnish the tape firmly before peeling off its backing paper. If this is awkward to peel, use the point of a craft knife or a pin, pushed into the backing strip at one end, to lift it. If your scissor blades become gummed up when trimming double-sided sticky tape, clean them with a rag dampened with white spirit.

CLEAR ADHESIVE TAPE

This can be used on the reverse side of butt-joined paper. Again, it is more successful when used with thinner paper and is best avoided where a piece is intended to be on permanent display as the tape may go brittle, discolour and lose its tack with age. You will also need to ensure all the tape joins are hidden.

Clear adhesive tape saddles are another quick way of joining paper, more suited to temporary sculptures for the reason given above. A small roll of clear sticky tape is made with the sticky side facing outwards. The more the 'saddles' are pressed down between two sheets, the flatter the join becomes.

ADHESIVE FOAM PADS

Double-sided adhesive foam pads are a manufactured equivalent of 'saddles'. These also act as spacers, creating a small space between two sheets of paper the width of the foam, and this effect can be increased by putting two or three together.

I find clear adhesive tape, its double-sided

cousin and adhesive pads most useful for temporary sculptures, which will not be subjected to extremes of heat or humidity, both of which may affect the adhesive properties of these products.

MASKING TAPE

Masking tape is excellent for temporary fastening of rough work which is to be taken apart and used for templates. If the tape is too tacky reduce this by sticking it on to your clothes a few times before you use it. Mark where each section of a sculpture fits together before you remove staples or tape. On a complicated paper sculpture, numbering the parts as you remove them for templates will allow you to reverse this order when you construct the finished work.

INTERLOCKING

Paper pieces can be joined without glue or tape by interlocking the parts. Slits cut halfway in each piece will hold together, three-dimensionally, when pushed into each other. Tabs may have to be planned for, before the making stage, to allow for the extra pieces of paper needed. However these, with corresponding slits, will work well, especially where they are held in place after insertion with a spot of glue. Many different kinds of interlocking joints are possible and Bruce Angrave, a pioneer of paper sculpture in this country, created a brilliant series of faces of famous people using the interlocking principle exclusively, eschewing glue and other forms of fastening in the construction.

STAPLES

Staples are a quick and easy way of joining but too many of them can look messy if they show on the outside of the work. However, they are ideal for holding together rough work and patterns, because they can be removed relatively easily to disassemble an experimental piece. Staples can also be used on supporting strips and constructional parts which will be hidden once the sculpture is completed.

GUN TACKER

A gun tacker, which fires staples into a card or wood base, can also be used to join paper quickly to its background. Again, for perfectionists, the proviso is that the tacking staples are hidden when the final layers of the sculpture are applied.

SPACING PAPER

Spacers are contructional pieces of paper, card or other materials used both to join and separate (that is, create a space in between) two sections of a paper sculpture to add to its three-dimensional effect. These spacers can be in the form of strips, various tabs, fan-folded paper, corrugated card, paper or plastic straws, paper rolls and cylinders. Of these, I find rolls and cylinders the most versatile. Subtle adjustment of the spacing can be made by squashing a cylinder slightly before or after it is in place, and heavier paper or thin card can be used to increase support and rigidity.

CORRUGATED CARD

Corrugated card can be used in a similar way to the adhesive foam pads mentioned above, by gluing one or more pieces between sheets to hold them apart. Its advantages are that it can be cut to any size or shape before gluing, it is cheap and easy to obtain and the corrugated side can be curved to fit on a round surface.

WHITE CARD

Thick white card can be used similarly to the corrugated variety and, with white paper sculpture, has the advantage of not showing through the sheets. If you need to curve it, use a former to roll it round.

FAN-FOLDED SPACERS

Fan-folded paper is a home-made equivalent of currugated card, the width of the fold determining the spacing between sheets. Fan-folded spacers, made from the same paper as your sculpture, are very strong once glued into place and are simple to use on curved surfaces.

PAPER & CARD STRIPS

Paper or card strips need to be of a reasonable thickness if used edge-on as spacers. The thickness allows you to apply glue to the edge and thicker strips have less tendency to buckle under the weight of the sheets above.

PAPER & CARD TABS

With a little ingenuity, all sorts of tabs can be devised as spacers from paper the same weight as your work, but the wider the spacing the stronger these need to be.

ROLLS & CYLINDERS

Paper straws are not easy to obtain now but plastic ones can also be used to join and space work, held in place with PVA glue. Paper straws are merely a manufactured equivalent of paper rolls which you can make yourself. Unlike straws, rolls can be home-made in an infinite variety of diameters and lengths. Make sure you use thin paper which rolls easily. Making their big brothers, cylinders, is covered in Project 1. Cylinders are the most versatile of all and glued end-on will support a considerable weight of paper. Experience and practice will soon enable you to choose which kind of spacer to use in each sculptural situation.

SUPPORTS AND ARMATURES

Small three-dimensional sculptures are usually self-supporting, the basic construction being designed with this in mind. However, many large paper sculptures will need additional support as there is a limit to the amount of weight paper will hold, particularly with top-heavy pieces. Most types of support are quite simple.

ROLLS & CYLINDERS

Armatures can be made in one, or a combination of materials, depending on the size of the sculpture and the combined weight an armature will need to support. Small work can be strengthened with an inner cardboard lining or may rest on card rolls. Paper rolls and cylinders offer similar advantages of strength, combined with lightness and ease of fixing. I have used thick card cylinders for figures 5 m (16 ft) tall.

CANES

Bamboo garden canes and split canes are very versatile supports because they are light, yet strong, and can be joined together easily by tying, taping or gluing the ends into small paper or card rolls. Thicker bamboo can be joined using rigid plastic piping of the kind used for plumbing. Take care when handling green split canes as the colour is water-soluble, comes off easily on the hands and can be transferred inadvertently to the surface of your sculpture.

Crumpled paper, wound round a thin cane or wood support, can be used to increase its diameter if this is desirable. A life-size paper sculpture figure may need only one or two sturdy garden canes fixed into a suitable base to hold it securely upright.

A giant Father Christmas, three storeys high, fastened to the outside of an American building needed a great deal of steel scaffolding and timber to hold him up successfully and secure his body to the walls, but I doubt anyone reading this book will be planning to take on such a mammoth undertaking!

TIMBER & PLY

For large three-dimensional work I always construct an accurate model and then scale this up to full size. In this way, mistakes, adjustments and difficulties in construction can be ironed out before committing oneself to the finished piece. You will also avoid wasting good paper if you make a smaller, experimental piece first. Timber, plywood and an inner card skin are my usual choices of an effective support for creating paper sculptures up to 7 m (23 ft) high.

SHEET MATERIALS

Some paper sculptors use sheet materials such as plywood and rigid plastic to provide armatures for three-dimensional work. These thinner materials are usually tacked or glued to a length of timber which is, in its turn, fastened securely to a base. Because all paper is relatively light, this sheet material armature can be very simple. An electric jigsaw will enable the sculptor to cut these sheets easily and quickly.

BAS-RELIEF ARMATURES

Bas-relief sculptures are easiest to handle mounted on a rigid background and small ones can be glued direct onto this. Card, foam-core board, plywood, chipboard and plastic sheet are just a few of the possibilities. These same sheet materials will also provide a stiff backing for building on paper pieces.

COVERED SUPPORTS

When sculptures can only be viewed frontally, the colour and material of their support is less critical. Where the support may be seen, it will need covering or colouring to match the sculptural item. I usually cover supports and armatures for bas-relief work with the same paper used in constructing the sculpture itself.

A stiff backing sheet for a bas-relief sculpture can be made by tracing a simplified version of the original full size drawing, then cutting this out. Sufficient information should be obtained on the chosen shape to aid setting out the different parts of the work in their correct positions for a realistic appearance.

PLYWOOD & CHIPBOARD

Large bas-relief sculptures are best attached to a solid backing once they are completed. This aids packing, transport and display and helps protect the vulnerable paper from too much handling. Plywood and chipboard sheets in various grades are good backing materials and can be painted or covered with coloured paper, felt or hessian to contrast effectively with the white paper if this is used for the sculpture. Heraldic colours and their

variations seem to be the most suitable for this purpose.

SELF-TAPPING SCREWS

Bas-relief sculptures can be simply glued to their base but I prefer to use self-tapping screws, put in from the rear of the backing sheet. Several of these will hold a large sculpture in place and have the advantage that it can be easily re-positioned with minimum damage to either the sculpture or the background.

Where a complicated armature is needed for the sculpture the same self-tapping screws are an ideal solution to joining the wood-based and plastic sheet materials which are often used for advanced, large scale paper sculpture. An appropriate wood glue or plastic cement could also be used for this purpose but would need to be compatible with both materials.

SPACERS

Individual parts of a sculpture may occasionally need additional support because they are not glued directly to the paper below. In this case I would use spacers of various kinds which are described on page 27.

I confess here that most of my armatures are, in fact, fairly crudely constructed as I design them to be completely disguised by their outer paper skin once the sculpture is complete and they are therefore built to be purely serviceable – their appearance is unimportant.

Each sculpture will, of course, dictate its own individual requirements for an armature, which may vary according to where it will be displayed, whether it needs to be free-standing or not, the weight of the paper it supports and so on. Whatever the many different factors affecting your particular choice of support, do try and keep it as simple as possible.

DISPLAY AND EXHIBITION

Paper sculpture is normally so light-weight that displaying pieces for your own pleasure, or showing them in public and educational venues is simplicity itself.

One of the first considerations is whether sculptures will be in place temporarily, for a few hours or days, exhibited for a longer period or, indeed, planned as a permanent exhibition. A decision on the time span of the display will often determine the method which can most appropriately be used for fixing the sculptures.

Temporary display of small bas-relief pieces is easy using a gun tacker to fasten them to an appropriate background. Household mapping, panel and drawing pins (white ones for preference), used discreetly, are also a very quick way of fastening sculptures to a backing board. The use of pins or staples will allow work to be removed easily, particularly useful in school or for seasonal decorations that are to be taken down and stored for another year.

ADHESIVE TAPES & FOAM PADS

Clear adhesive tape 'saddles', double-sided tape and adhesive pads are also useful for temporary display, but are more liable to damage both sculpture and background when removed. Mouldable adhesive can be used similarly but will tend to leave a slight mark on walls and work. Its tackiness increases with age so take care as it can remove paint from some surfaces.

Right: The Three Kings were commissioned from the author by the Isle of Man Post Office for their 1991 Christmas stamps.

SELF-ADHESIVE FABRIC
(VELCRO)

Self-adhesive fabric squares, circles or strips are another useful innovation for holding light pieces firmly in place while they are on temporary display. These provide the advantage of allowing a slight adjustment in the position of the sculpture and allowing it to be removed easily, although there still remains the problem of the piece stuck to the support.

Make sure that all the surfaces and the situation are dry as damp affects these adhesives, reducing their tack.

NYLON MONOFILAMENT
& COTTON THREAD

Nylon fishing line, which is available in a wide range of breaking strains, is superb for suspending three-dimensional sculptures, though you may have to consult a fishing guide to learn which knots are the best to use with this slippery customer. A spot of strong glue will help secure each knot against slipping. Cotton thread for sewing makes a fair, but weaker, substitute and is not so invisible.

GLUES

Medium-sized bas-relief work mounted on card can be fixed to its background with clear, solvent-based adhesive. A hot-glue gun also works well, the hot adhesive setting solid very quickly. The decision to use glues will depend on the nature of the background you are attaching the sculpture to, the amount of adjustment which may be needed in positioning a work and the permanency of the fixing required. Both these glues are permanent when set and will damage the support and the sculpture if it is removed.

SCREWS

Large-scale bas-relief sculptures need fixing firmly to their backgrounds. I have generally used a plywood armature for these so I can put self-tapping screws in from the front or through into the

ply from the rear of the background. Screws, or indeed any other hardware, must be invisible from the front of the work so you may need a couple of suitably placed sculptural details to cover the screwheads once the fastening is completed for a perfect finish.

SPACING

Many relief sculptures need spacing away from their backgrounds. I use greyboard cylinders, set vertically, for small items and wooden blocks for larger works. Even on a large piece you may not need to use more than four or five wooden spacers. Keep the blocks as few, as small and as light as possible because they are only for spacing and fixing. Cord can be fastened to screw-eyes in two horizontal spacing blocks and the whole sculpture hung on picture hooks.

Hundreds of different sorts of fastenings are available in hardware stores and builder's merchants, some of which may prove suitable for the particular job you are doing. The position the sculpture is in and the kind of background it needs to be fixed to will usually dictate your choice of fastening. Remember that plain coloured backgrounds work best with most paper sculpture.

THREE-DIMENSIONAL
WORK

Three-dimensional sculptures are often self-supporting and, if not, will probably have been built on an armature fixed into a base of ply or chipboard. Usually three-dimensional works need to be raised clear of the floor to be seen at their best. This can be done simply by setting them on a table covered with a plain coloured cloth, which reaches to the floor, or by using exhibition plinths of the correct height.

LIGHTING

Whether bas-relief or fully three-dimensional, all paper sculptures look best when properly lit. Good lighting creates strong shadows and highlights and gives the appearance of real solidity and three-dimensionality to the ephemeral paper.

You will need to experiment for yourself with lighting positions, but a good general rule for both single and multiple light sources is to have them angled at 45° from one side only. This type of lighting is much more dramatic with white sculpture because nearly all the light is reflected from the paper surface. If your lighting is portable try a number of different options and choose the one which reveals most of the details and textures on your sculpture.

Coloured floods or spots can be used to add to the mood of the piece and, again, this option works best with white paper.

STORAGE

Once the exhibition is over, paper sculpture must be stored away from its two worst enemies – dust and damp. Clear polythene bags and sheets are unbeatable for this and, because you can see through the material, you will be able to avoid damage when handling packed work. Clear adhesive tape and self-adhesive parcel tape both hold well on polythene and will seal bags successfully. Dust can be blown, brushed or hoovered very

carefully from sculptures before storage. Kept dry, and at room temperature, in well-sealed bags paper sculptures can be stored successfully for many years.

If you handle many pieces for exhibition purposes it is well worth investing in a pair of thin, white cotton gloves. Wearing these avoids any chance of marking the paper with greasy or sweaty fingermarks during handling.

FRAMES & CASES

The traditional way to preserve small bas-relief paper sculptures is to mount them in a deep frame glazed with either glass or clear plastic. Small three dimensional works used to be protected by bell-jars sealed to a wooden base, but most sculptors working today use perspex boxes to achieve the same ends – keeping out dust, damp and insects.

A final word, which is a personal one: don't leave paper works on show until they get very dusty, damaged and sad looking. Two of paper's loveliest qualities are its pristine surface and its ephemerality. Consign all aged work to the two rest homes for old paper – the dustbin or the fire!

Left: The author sculpted this cased and glazed Black Horse for Lloyds Bank, Isle of Man

PAPER SCULPTURE IN EDUCATION

As I intimated in *Making A Start*, a crucial factor for artists, sculptors and creative people in all walks of life is the ability to perceive with the right hemisphere of the brain (cognitive shift).

Generally, we use the brain's left hemisphere, which is symbolic, verbal and logical with drawing ability limited to symbols. We all know adults who still draw in a childlike manner and protest they have no talent in this direction. Our right hemisphere, in contrast, processes information holistically (all at once), spatially, inspirationally, in great detail and has immense artistic ability.

Drawing is important because it underpins most sculpture, and certainly paper sculpture. It allows the world to be seen differently than in normal perception and it allows you to achieve the cognitive shift from the left brain (L-mode) to right brain (R-mode) of seeing our world.

Although I have deliberately kept drawing requirements to a minimum throughout this book, if you want to design and make your own paper sculptures, drawing skills are invaluable.

Two of the delights of being in R-mode are that the constant chatter of everyday thoughts seems to go away and that the right hemisphere has no sense of time, so this flies by very pleasurably. All sculptural, three-dimensional activities have the advantage that the cognitive shift is produced automatically because we work spatially with our medium.

An advantage of paper sculpture is that it is very economical in equipment and material costs. In addition, there are only five basic techniques to learn and the shapes you need to construct are simple too, with cylinders, cuboids and cones being the three main forms.

Suitable for all ages and abilities, paper sculpture can be used for Art Therapy, with the disadvantaged and the handicapped, because its practice is absorbing and increases manipulative skills. In addition, even the simplest projects produce spectacular results.

In its guise as paper engineering the ease with which it can be manipulated, joined, cut, changed and combined with other materials encourages a practical, problem-solving approach among students. In addition, modular construction with cylinders, cuboids and strips, as in Projects 1, 2 and 8, offers a real challenge to would be designers in paper.

With limited resources available to schools and similar educational establishments paper sculpture is suitably economical and paper's lightness, strength and availability lends itself to exhibition work, displays and murals. Large work in this medium is as easy to create as small pieces.

Whenever I take a school class or public workshop I invariably use white paper for the sculptures because I believe this encourages a three dimensional approach. Often children will stick coloured images flat on to each other, the difference in colour revealing the form. When using white on white this is not possible, and only spacing or shaping creates the shadows and highlights to separate one piece from another.

DISPLAY SHEET

Concentrate on the five basic techniques when teaching children. My own approach is to talk about each technique in turn and then to get each child to do a display sheet containing the five in practical form.

Supply each student with a coloured A4 ($8^{1}/4$ x $11^{3}/4$ in) sheet placed Flats way up (portrait) and ask them to write down the five techniques, top left as you introduce each topic to them. An A3 ($11^{3}/4$ x $16^{1}/2$ in) white sheet, also Flats way round (portrait), is then folded and cut four times to give five rectangles of paper, the smallest two pieces being identical. Stack them as you fold and cut each, in order of size, with the smallest on top.

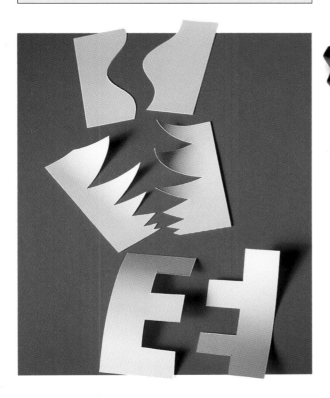

CUT

Take one of these small pieces and cut it once from bottom to top. This cut may be straight, curved, wiggly or jagged, as long as there is only one; no trimming or neatening is allowed. These two pieces are stuck down on the coloured sheet, slightly apart so that the space between them is a connecting space, making a negative design. Put PVA down the long, straight sides with a cocktail stick so that you are free to bend up the cut edges if you wish to do so. Attach this and the other four sculptural examples in any position you wish on the coloured paper. They can partly overlap the coloured paper or even connect each other.

FOLD

Fan-fold the second small rectangle, starting Flats way up (portrait) keeping the first overlap to about 1 cm (¹/2 in) wide. When the folding is complete, see how many different ways you can manipulate this unit before you glue it down. It can be laid flat, stood up on one edge, fastened at one end into a fan, folded in the middle to make a bow tie, bent right round and joined to make a star shape at its ends, stuck down both sides like a curved, corrugated roof or on one side to make a set of steps. These are just a few of the possibilities for a fan-folded piece of paper – I wonder if you can discover more?

CURL

Cut strips in your next size of paper: three medium ones, four thin ones and the remainder divided into three separate strips. Keep the medium and thin strips as two units, leaving them joined at the top, stopping your cuts about 1 cm (¹/2 in) from the upper edge of the paper. Hold your paper Flats way up (portrait) and cut the strips carefully, as parallel and evenly as you can, and from the opposite side to the one you are holding. This avoids all the awkwardness of cutting near to your fingers.

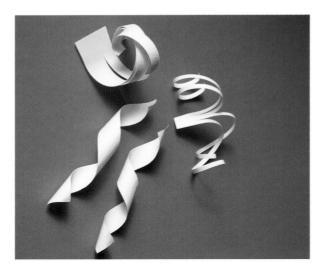

Use scissors to curl the three medium strips, being careful to support these at the joined end as you pull them. Use a pencil for curling if you find this technique difficult with scissors. When curling the four fine strips, do two to the left and two to the right. Notice how the fine ones curl tighter and are even slightly spiral if you angle the scissors. Bend a tab on the base of the four strip unit so that it looks rather like a little waterspout when it is glued on.

Two of the three strips you have left need to be wound, one at a time, round a pencil, starting at the top and spiralling downwards in a movement akin to twiddling your hair around your fingers. Pull each strip tightly round the pencil, then release it and you will have two spirals or ringlets to add to your coloured sheet.

BEND

Take the spare third strip, holding half in each hand, fingers upwards, thumbs underneath, and stroke one end of this, pulling it through your hand. As you stroke the paper, turn your wrist so that the strip curves over the thumb of your moving hand. Bend the other end of the strip in the opposite direction to make an 'S', then lay PVA along its edge with a cocktail stick. Glue it in place, edge on.

SCORE

Draw a wriggling snake, in pencil, on your penultimate sheet. Keep the snake on the plump side with a head and pointed tail, avoiding any loops in the body. When you have cut it out, turn it over to hide the pencil marks, and score from the head end right down the centre of the body with a craft knife or compasses. Try to turn the snake rather than the craft knife as you score its body. Crease the scoreline carefully, remembering that the curves you create will be tighter once creasing is complete. Snip a mouth in the head and add a tongue and eye if you wish, then glue the snake to your coloured sheet by its tail.

Above: David Swinton making a Floor Piece for an art class at the Buchan School, Isle of Man.

FLOOR PIECES

At the end of the day the work area and floor space are often covered with scraps of paper in all kinds of shapes and sizes. I make Floor Pieces with these bits of paper, attaching them freely to a cylinder or cuboid support. Work as spontaneously and quickly as you can to make your floor piece, which can then be suspended, so that it is free to revolve, maybe in the light from a nearby window.

Often the abstract sculptures will have a completely different character to the usual representational, decorative work. You may be able to encourage some of your students to try this approach again, expressing themselves directly through the shapes and forms they choose to create.

It is said we humans have had a special relationship with the four elements – earth, air, fire and water – from ancient times. In our modern world, I'm sure we can add paper as a fifth element.

A PERSONAL STYLE

Make a display of your finished reference sheets by pinning them together on a board. This is a useful exercise in appreciating the individuality which can be achieved even when working within strict guidelines. Teachers and parents should feel free to invent their own variations on the theme of cut, fold, curl, bend and score.

You will have noticed that there is a single sheet left over from our original set of five. Fold this in half, Flats way round (portrait), and cut it in two. Curl half into a cylinder, long and thin or short and fat, and decorate it using the spare piece of paper. It's always a good idea, at the end of a period of strictly directed work, to give children the freedom to express themselves individually with paper sculpture.

When I work with a group, introducing paper sculpture in this way, I demonstrate each technique while the children watch. They then complete the same task, returning to my table when they are ready for the next demonstration.

FINGER PUPPET

(BASIC CONSTRUCTION: CYLINDERS AND SPHERES)

EQUIPMENT & MATERIALS

A4 (8¹/4 x 11³/4 in) white paper – several sheets
Pencils and soft eraser
Scissors • PVA glue • cocktail sticks

Finger Puppet: 13 cm (5 in) approx.

Paper sculpture is at its most effective when simple shapes are used for the main structure and decorative detail is superimposed on these to create the character of the piece. Two of the most useful basic shapes are cylinders and cuboids (or cubes). Spheres are difficult to construct successfully and paper sculptors usually try to avoid them by substituting several small, curved shapes to form the basic structure of the sculpture and also to give the appearance of an underlying dome. The final piece will be just as successful and effective as if a sphere had been used.

Glue an overlap
of 1/2 in (1 cm)

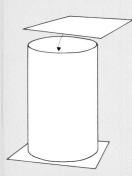

Apply glue to
edges to secure
base and top

CYLINDERS

I use cylinders more than any other three-dimensional form in my own work because they are such versatile spacers and supports and can be cut, overlapped and re-joined to provide a tremendous variety of complicated head and body shapes. Mechanical parts, such as wheels and cogs, can also be classed as modified cylinders.

Most cylinders are formed by the curling technique – small ones with scissors and larger ones rolled over the sharp edge of a table. Very large sheets of paper will not need curling before they are made into cylinders. Keep the overlap for gluing the two sides together minimal – about 1 cm (1/2 in) for small work.

When cylinders need to be closed at one or both ends, put glue around the chosen, circular edge – a cocktail stick is an ideal applicator – and gently press a slightly larger piece of paper on to this. Leave the piece until absolutely dry, then trim off the excess paper as closely to the cylinder as is possible, repeating the process to seal the opposite end.

Edge tabs can join bases and tops if you prefer, but these are fiddly to cut, awkward to glue and generally lumpy in use.

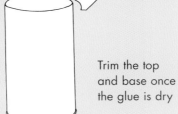

Trim the top
and base once
the glue is dry

Curling narrow pieces of paper is well nigh impossible so, when you need thin cylinders, curl a longer piece of paper and cut whatever width you require from it once the curling process is complete. A former of similar diameter will help support your narrow cylinder as you glue it. Remember to apply glue to the edge which overlaps, not the inside edge!

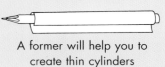

A former will help you to
create thin cylinders

ROLLS

Paper rolls, although technically cylinders, differ in that they are usually much thinner and the rolling process overlaps the paper to make a stronger unit. Paper for rolls does not need to be pre-curled. Roll from one diagonal corner to the other as tightly as you can before gluing the loose end in place at the centre. It takes a bit of practice to make a tight roll so have several sheets of paper at hand the first time you try this skill. The thin ends will need to be trimmed slightly into the firm part of the roll before use.

Tight paper roll – roll paper diagonally

Most of the rolls I use are made from 80 gsm photocopying or typing paper. If rolls taper slightly as you make them you will find it easy to glue the thin end of one inside the wider end of the next and so on, thus extending the overall length.

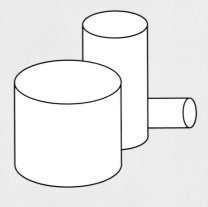

SPHERES

A paper sphere would have to be moulded from pulp for it to be perfect so, in paper sculpture, we must be content with making the best approximations to this shape. Paper sculptors approach this problem in many ways but two of the simpler ones are given here:

SPHERE 1

A crude sphere can be made from eight paper strips of identical width and length. The width should be one eighth of the circumference of the sphere needed. Allowing a 1 cm (1/2 in) overlap, bend and glue together four of the strips to make four circles. Stick two of these circles together at right angles to each other. Glue the next two circles inside these to bisect the openings. Fasten the last four strips together to fill the gaps, after curling them round the sphere. Again you will find a cocktail stick just the right tool for applying a tiny dot of glue top and bottom.

Eight identical strips form the sphere

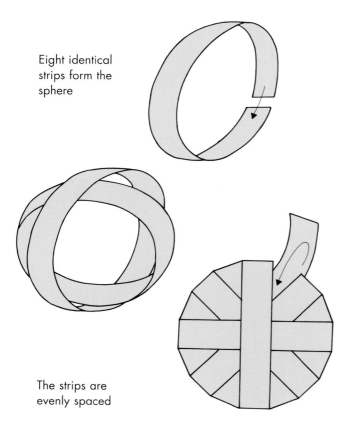

The strips are evenly spaced

SPHERE 2

Another, more accurate, way of creating a sphere is to make an internal armature to support segments of paper which can be glued on one at a time. The armature consists of a paper roll with a disc glued centrally on to it. The width of this disc and the length of the roll must be identical and represent the diameter of your chosen sphere. The desired number of identical segments, each shaped like a leaf or a slice of peel cut from an orange, is glued to the top and bottom of the roll, which has small cardboard discs attached to facilitate the process (see diagrams). As you work round the sphere, one side of each segment is glued to the preceding piece.

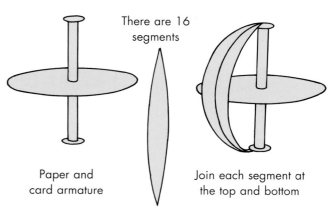

There are 16 segments

Paper and card armature

Join each segment at the top and bottom

Segment shapes can be produced by guess work and trial and error, or can be made by constructing an oblong half the length of the circumference and of a width which represents the correct numerical division of this circumference. Once this box is constructed, the half-segment can be drawn inside it and used as a template for as many as are needed.

Many artists have used polystyrene or table tennis balls for the heads of their paper figures and this is a simple way to achieve a perfect sphere which is light enough to use with paper and easily glued with PVA. Be sure that the white of your paper matches that of the plastic.

As you will see later in the book, most of the projects avoid spherical shapes which are particularly awkward to create in full three dimensions. However, an awareness of this problem will nearly always lead to a solution as you enjoy paper sculpture and become more proficient in manipulating your chosen material.

MAKE A FINGER PUPPET

Have fun with cylinders making a finger-puppet. Glue the neck cylinder inside the head one, keeping both joins at the back. Invent and add eyes, nose, mouth, eyebrows, ears and hair in this order. Make sure that you manipulate each piece of paper three-dimensionally so that the features give sculptural expression to the face. Stick on the hair last so that it covers the hole at the top of the head. This is done most easily by gluing two paper strips inside the head cylinder at right angles to each other. These strips will form attachment points for the hair as you glue it on, working from bottom to top as you would slate a roof, ending at the crown of the head. Keep the curvature of these support strips shallow because the top of the head is quite flat. Finger puppets look excellent in white or coloured paper but remember to express all the characteristic details in paper and don't be tempted to add these in pencil, pen or felt-tip pen – the result will not be nearly as effective as the paper version.

LANTERN AND LETTERBOX

(BASIC CONSTRUCTION:
CUBE AND CUBOID)

EQUIPMENT & MATERIALS

A4 (8¹/4 x 11³/4 in) white paper – two sheets
PVA glue • Cocktail stick
Small craft knife • Cutting mat
30 cm (1ft) Plastic rule • Steel rule
Pencil • Soft eraser
Nylon monofilament or cotton thread
Tracing paper • Paper clips (two)

Finished size: 20 cm (8 in) approx.

The lantern and letterbox are both constructed from a basic cuboid. (The same principles of construction apply to making a cube.) For both decorations, start by following these instructions for making a cuboid:

CUBOID

Take a rectangular sheet of paper, place Flats way round (portrait), folding and creasing so that approximately 1 cm (¹/2 in) of paper is left showing. Turn the piece round and fold over the 1cm (¹/2 in) overlap to

Any rectangle
of paper

Fold, leaving
1 cm (¹/2in) showing

42

form a flap. Lift the flap upright, turn the piece again and fold the doubled paper to touch this flap. Carefully open the paper up and close your cuboid by reversing the fold on the open side. Imagine closing the lid on Pandora's Box!

Fold over this flap

Glue the flap on the outside and then fold it down flat, pressing down the loose side firmly on top of it to stick the two sides together. Leave until the glue sets before opening up the cuboid by gently pressing two of its outside edges.

Fold doubled side to flap

A top and base can be added by gluing the upper edge of your cuboid and placing a slightly larger square of paper on this wet edge, turning the box upside down and repeating this process to close the other end. The top and base must be absolutely dry before you trim them as closely as you can to the cuboid. This method of attaching top and base is not only quicker but also more successful than trying to make a square of the correct size to join on with tabs.

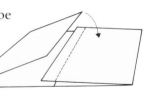

Open out reverse fold open side

Uneven, hollow shapes, even those with a gently undulating edge, can all be completed in this manner, provided that the edge runs in an unbroken curve.

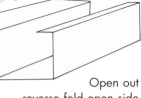

Lay flat and glue together

Cubes are made in precisely the same way, but the rectangle of paper needs careful measurement to ensure its length is four times its width plus an additional 1 cm (1/2 in) for the overlap. Mark this flap accurately before folding up the cube.

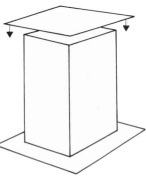

Add top and base if desired

DECORATIVE LANTERN

You will need to make a tall, open-ended cuboid for your lantern. Fold it flat and then make cuts from each opposite edge. These cuts must fall slightly short of the first quarter of the total width and can be in any direction and of any even number (see diagrams). It is probably best to start with a few straight cuts and then progress to angled and curved ones; you can create a more intricate effect by increasing their number.

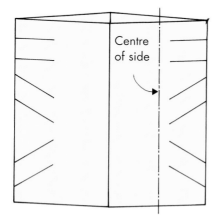

Centre of side

Make an even number of cuts on each side

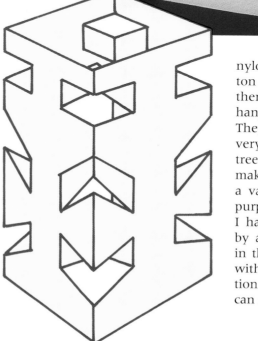

Once two opposite sides are complete, flatten the cuboid at right angles to the first cuts so that the other two sides can be dealt with in a similar fashion. Opposite edges need to match each other exactly for the best results, but alternate sides can differ if you wish to use two different designs.

To make the lantern, leave the top edge as it is and push the second section in the first side firmly into the lantern, creasing the edges to make a sharp fold, thus reversing it. Reverse fold every other section on the first side, leaving the bottom edge unfolded to match the top. Repeat this process with the other three sides of the lantern to complete the sculpture.

These lanterns look most effective when suspended from nylon monofilament or cotton thread, especially when there is a whole row of them hanging together in a display. They are also excellent in very small sizes as Christmas tree decorations – you could make them all in white or in a variety of colours for this purpose. The smallest lantern I have ever seen was made by a schoolgirl who pushed in the tiny reversed sections with a pin. Have a competition to see how small you can make one!

LETTERBOXES

When you make letter boxes cut out the spaces in between the letters before you glue the cuboid together. I usually draw the letters back to front on the inside of each face, starting with a single line and then doubling it.

An easier way is to use tracing paper cut to the size of one face of your cuboid. Plan your letters the correct way round within a border of 0.5 –1 cm (1/4–1/2 in), overlapping the letters slightly so they are joined here and there to each other and to the border round the edges. Reverse the tracing on to each inside face of the  cuboid by going over your letters with a pencil or ballpoint pen, or burnish down the tracing with the smooth handle of a teaspoon to transfer the image on to the paper. If you use a soft 2B pencil for tracing the letters you will be able to burnish the image down very easily and repeat it as many times as you need. A few scraps of masking tape will stop the tracing paper from moving about while you trace or burnish.

When you have completed the tracings of your reversed letters, cut out all the spaces between and within letters with a small craft knife. Remember to use a cutting board under your paper. Once the cutting is complete, clip your letterbox together temporarily with two paper clips while you mark with a pencil any places along the 1 cm (1/2 in) overlap which show behind the letters and must be cut away before gluing. Complete this job before removing the paper clips and finally fastening the overlap in place to finish your letterbox.

Once you are proficient at drawing and cutting out letters, try coloured or decorated papers or thin card. Occasionally, I have been able to dispense with the border altogether and allow the letters to link and support themselves. This approach made the usual long joint impractical and I dispensed with it entirely, using several small tabs instead, positioned inside the cuboid, to close it and join one letter to another along the open edge.

Letterboxes make ideal greetings cards with an appropriate message for birthdays, Christmas or any other special occasions and, of course, easily fold flat to be slipped into an envelope.

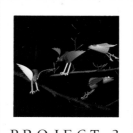

LITTLE BIRD

*(BASIC CONSTRUCTION:
CONE)*

~

EQUIPMENT & MATERIALS

*A5 (5⁷/8 x 8¹/4 in) white or coloured paper –
two sheets
Pencil • Scissors
PVA glue • Cocktail stick
Compasses ·
Thin wire (optional)
Pliers (optional)
Cotton thread or nylon monofilament
Darning needle (optional)
Small piece of stiff card (optional)*

Finished size: 13 cm (5 in) approx.

This dainty little three-dimensional bird, based on a cone, can be made in a flying or perching version. I generally make mine out of A5 (5⁷/8 x 8¹/4 in) paper although larger models will be just as successful. A group of children can easily create a flock in a couple of hours. A cone is the most difficult of the three basic forms to construct so don't be discouraged if you can't get its point completely closed.

CONE

Cut segment

Draw a quarter segment of a circle and cut it out. Hold the point towards you, keeping this still, while curling the wide end over the edge of a table to relax the paper. Remember to pinch the point once this process is completed, then roll up the paper to make the cone, holding it in one hand while the other hand twists the cone as tightly as possible. Shaping the cone in this way

Relax the paper makes the gluing easier.

Stick the two edges together by applying glue to the overlapping one. Hold the join face down on the table top while you stick it, carefully pushing your fingers or a pencil inside the cone to hold it while the glue dries. To make a cone with a perfect point takes practise and if you don't succeed this time there is no need to worry as we will be cutting a beak into the pointed end of this one.

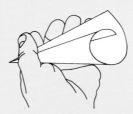

Roll up tightly

Allow the glue to dry thoroughly, then turn the cone so its join is at the bottom and pinch the sides of the point to flatten it. It is easier to cut the 'V' of the bird's beak out of a pinched point. Open your scissors wide to do this, as snipping with the ends of the blades makes a ragged job.

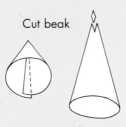

Support in hand

Cut beak

Position the cone on a table, overlap and glue underneath edges, keeping a forefinger or pencil inside to hold overlap

WINGS

Fold a suitable rectangle of paper in half Houses way round (landscape) and cut out both wings together. Size, shape, feathers, colour and so on will be a matter of personal choice.

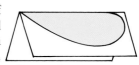

Cut out the wings

Several straight cuts at the ends of the wings will make simple feathers, but you may wish to make separate feathers and build them up in layers for a more authentic finish. Put the wings to one side to be glued on later.

Cut feathers

EYES

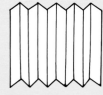

The eyes are simply circles with a slit cut to the centre, overlapped and glued. They will need pupils which are smaller circles, with a 'V' cut out of the sides. These are held in place with two tiny blobs of PVA, top and bottom.

TAIL

Fanfold a square or rectangle of paper and squeeze it together at the base to make a fan, then wind a scrap of clear adhesive tape round this base to secure it.

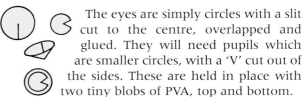

Fanfold shape

Decorate the tail by cutting into the folded section and curling it if you wish, then fasten its base inside the cone with clear adhesive tape.

Secure tail with sticky tape

Perching bird

LEGS AND FEET

Bend strips for legs

Cut two thin strips for legs, bending two tabs at the ends of these for the perching version.

Cut both feet out of a small folded rectangle of paper. Reduce the length of the two outside toes to match the middle one and curl all toes to make claws (see diagram below).

 Curl toes

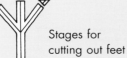
Stages for cutting out feet

If you wish you can cut the ends of the toes to a fine point before curling to make the claws more authentic.

Glue the eyes in place just back from the beak and the wings in position about halfway along the cone. Wings for the perching bird need to be fixed to the sides of the cone; the flying versions are glued on to its back. Stick the legs into the open end of the cone opposite the tail.

Complete the perching bird by cutting two pieces of thin wire (shape as in the diagram, right) and gluing them into the body and on to the back of the legs.

Wire legs

The wire 'claw' can then be fastened on to a suitable branch with the aid of pliers.

Insert cotton thread or fine nylon monofilament through the back of the flying bird at the point of balance to suspend it from the ceiling. I use a darning needle to insert my cotton thread or nylon line, making a large knot at one end and sewing a small piece of stiff card on to it first, to prevent the knot pulling through the thin paper.

Remember to increase the thickness of the paper if you wish to make larger versions of this appealing sculpture.

You will need to cut a small slit at the top of the open end of the cone to insert the tail for the perching version. Bend the base of this fan to one side when you are fastening it in place.

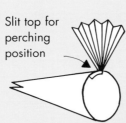
Slit top for perching position

Tail for flying bird

Flying bird

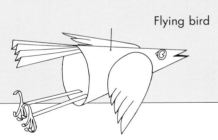

Try a group of multicoloured birds on a whitened or natural winter branch, with some 'flying' away across the room, for a very effective display.

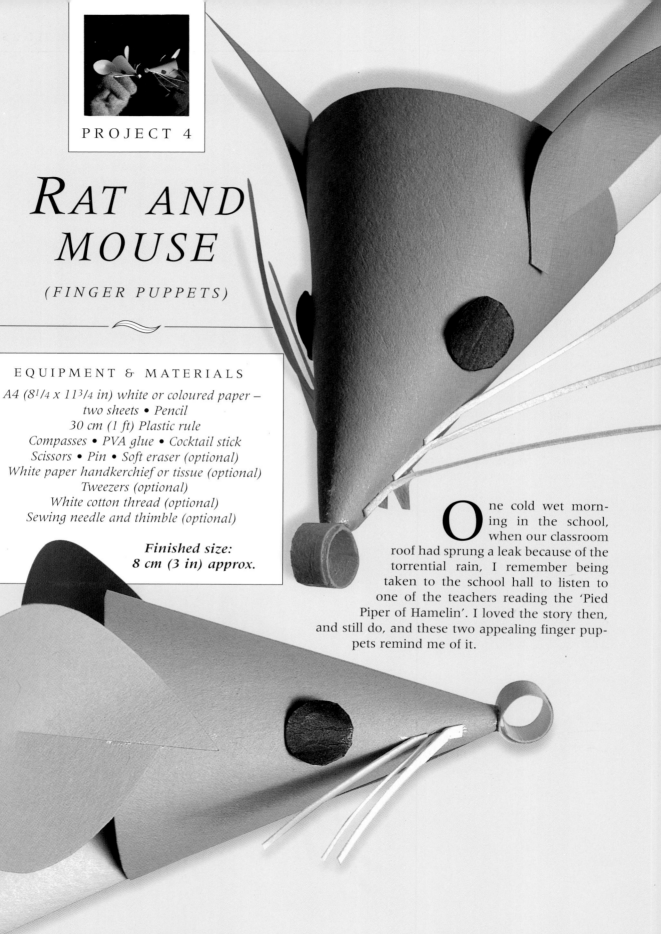

RAT AND MOUSE

(FINGER PUPPETS)

EQUIPMENT & MATERIALS

A4 (8¹/₄ x 11³/₄ in) white or coloured paper –
two sheets • Pencil
30 cm (1 ft) Plastic rule
Compasses • PVA glue • Cocktail stick
Scissors • Pin • Soft eraser (optional)
White paper handkerchief or tissue (optional)
Tweezers (optional)
White cotton thread (optional)
Sewing needle and thimble (optional)

Finished size:
8 cm (3 in) approx.

O ne cold wet morn-
ing in the school,
when our classroom
roof had sprung a leak because of the
torrential rain, I remember being
taken to the school hall to listen to
one of the teachers reading the 'Pied
Piper of Hamelin'. I loved the story then,
and still do, and these two appealing finger puppets remind me of it.

HEAD AND NECK

I prefer to make the rat and mouse at the same time as both their heads are based on small cones. Start by drawing a small circle of about 5 cm (2 in) in radius, cut it out and then cut it in two across the centre. Take one piece and make a tiny crease in the centre of the diameter. This will help you to cross over the two edges to make a cone. Wind the cone up as tightly as you can to relax the paper before gluing. Glue the overlapping edge sparingly and hold it in place once the little cone is the required width. Repeat with the other half circle of paper.

Cut a 5 cm (2 in) wide strip of paper, curl it into a plain cylinder to fit your forefinger and glue together at the overlap. Once the glue is dry, cut the cylinder in half to make one piece of 'neck' for each animal. Glue the 'neck' inside the cone, matching the two joins and keeping them both together at the bottom edge for a neat finish.

5 cm (2 in)

Make two
small cones

Make cylinder
and cut in half

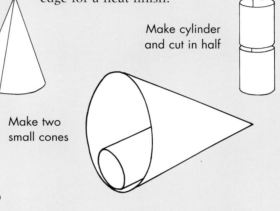

EARS

Study the diagrams with this project to see the differences in shape and size of rat and mouse ears, then cut these out of folded scraps of paper in pairs. You may draw them lightly in pencil first if you wish, but be sure to rub out any pencil lines before forming and gluing. If the ears are too large, trim them down carefully around the edges; if they are too small, make another pair. It's all valuable experience in confident cutting and judging shapes and sizes. Soon it will become second nature.

Once the ears are made, slit them from the middle of the straight end to their centre. Overlap and glue the two edges of the slit to give a hollow ear which will stick out from the head. Trim off any small ends from this overlap which spoil the line of the ear. Glue both ears on to the head, making sure you have a dry run first to mark their positions with a pencil dot.

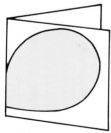

Mouse ears

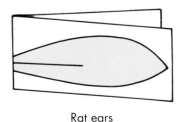

Rat ears

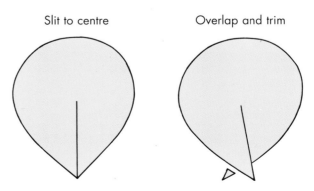

Slit to centre

Overlap and trim

NOSE

A very thin strip rolled and glued into a little ring will make a round nose for both rat and mouse. Trim the point off the head cone to make it easier to attach the nose.

Make two noses

EYES

Eyes are made in the usual way by cutting a slit to the centre of a small circle and overlapping and gluing the slit to make a shallow cone like a Chinese hat. A pupil with a little 'V' cut out of it is fastened inside this eye with a couple of tiny dots of PVA. Angle the eyes, and the 'V' in the pupil, towards the nose of the animal when you stick them on. Younger children of four to six years old may find it easier to make eyes by rolling two small balls of thin, white tissue paper.

Make four eyes

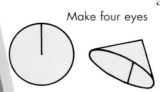

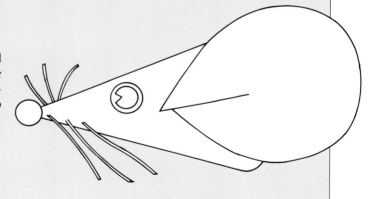

Both the rat and the mouse finger puppets have six whiskers. These need to be cut very finely and have a minute tab bent at one end so each whisker can be attached to the snout.

MAKE THE WHISKERS

The whiskers stick straight out on the mouse

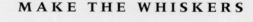

Cut twelve whiskers

Use the point of a pin to apply the PVA to each whisker and tweezers to place them in position. Tweezers are a useful aid when gluing on tiny details, especially for people with big fingers like myself! I allow the mouse's whiskers to stick straight out but angle the rat's set racily backwards.

It is possible to use three short lengths of white cotton and a needle to sew whiskers right through the snout, but these will be much floppier than the paper variety. Be sure to use a thimble for pushing your needle through or you may end up with a punctured finger and red and white sculpture! Trim all the cotton whiskers to the same length once they are in place.

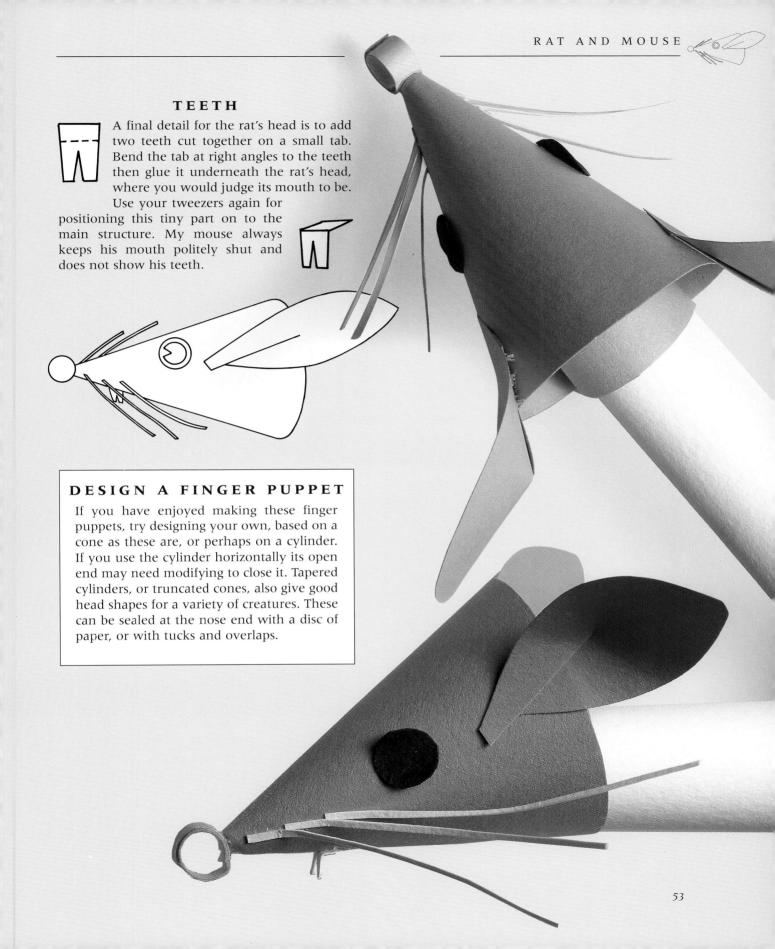

TEETH

A final detail for the rat's head is to add two teeth cut together on a small tab. Bend the tab at right angles to the teeth then glue it underneath the rat's head, where you would judge its mouth to be.

Use your tweezers again for positioning this tiny part on to the main structure. My mouse always keeps his mouth politely shut and does not show his teeth.

DESIGN A FINGER PUPPET

If you have enjoyed making these finger puppets, try designing your own, based on a cone as these are, or perhaps on a cylinder. If you use the cylinder horizontally its open end may need modifying to close it. Tapered cylinders, or truncated cones, also give good head shapes for a variety of creatures. These can be sealed at the nose end with a disc of paper, or with tucks and overlaps.

LOG RAFT

EQUIPMENT & MATERIALS

A4 (8¹/4 x 11³/4 in) white paper – three sheets
Scissors • Small craft knife
PVA glue • Pencil • Soft eraser
White cotton thread
Sheet of sea blue paper (optional)

Finished size: 20 cm (8 in) approx.

Rafts always conjure up romantic visions in my mind of shipwrecked sailors trying to escape some remote palm-fringed island but, in fact, the reality of life on such a vessel may have been very different. The French artist, Theodore Gericault's most celebrated work, the *Raft of the Medusa* depicts the harrowing ordeal suffered by victims of a terrible shipwreck that was a major political scandal of its day.

Still used in some parts of the world, rafts are made by lashing several logs together to form a bouyant platform. An epic, modern voyage was made by Thor Heyerdahl and five companions in 1947 on the balsa-wood raft *KON-TIKI*, when they sailed from Callao, Peru to Tuamotu Island in the South Pacific.

RAFT

Begin your raft by making five identical, thin cylinders or 'logs'. You will get four of these from an A4 (8¼ x 11¾ in) sheet (see diagrams). It is usually very difficult to curl a thin piece of paper across its width so I advise curling the whole A4 (8¼ x 11¾ in) sheet then cutting this into four smaller sections. Roll the pieces tightly, pulling the edges apart slightly to apply glue to the overlapping one. Keep the glued overlap, of about 1 cm (½ in), on the table and roll the other edge on to it.

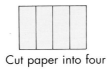

Cut paper into four

Glue logs together

Once made, the five cylinders need fastening together in some way. They can be simply glued to each other, or paper strips can be added top and bottom, fore and aft to the raft. You can also join your logs in other ways and the diagrams illustrate some of the options.

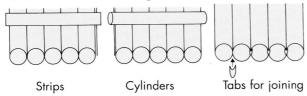

Strips   Cylinders   Tabs for joining

SAIL

Next cut a sail of a suitable size, with a concave lower margin, and curve this gently over the edge of your table before gluing its top to the yard arm.

Cut sail
Glue to yard

Curve sail

A quicker way to attach the sail and dispense with the yard arm altogether is to cut two slits in a cross shape in the top centre of the sail and then slide the mast through this, gluing them together once they are in the desired position.

Cross slits in top of sail

MAST AND YARD ARM

Roll a mast from a thin sheet of A4 (8¼ x 11¾ in) typing or photocopying paper and trim both ends once the roll has been glued together. Cut two small slits, in a cross shape, in the centre of the middle log, push the mast into this cross and glue in place.

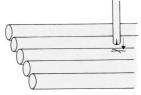

Glue mast into centre log

Make a yard arm by rolling thin paper in the same way as before, and tie it on near the top of the mast with cotton thread. A tiny dot of glue will secure the knot and stop it slipping.

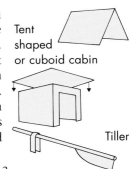

Pencil supports log while glue dries

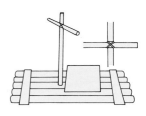

Add yard arm and tie in place

SHELTER OR CABIN

Fold a rectangle of paper in half for a simple tentlike shelter or make a cuboid, adding a top and cutting out windows and doors for a more sophisticated cabin. Fasten this to the logs with small L-shaped paper tabs fixed at intervals around the cabin base.

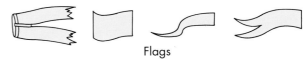

Tent shaped or cuboid cabin

Tiller

Other details such as a tiller, flags, sea-chest, cotton rigging and even a shipwrecked sailor can be added too.

Flags

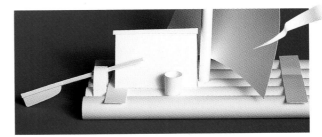

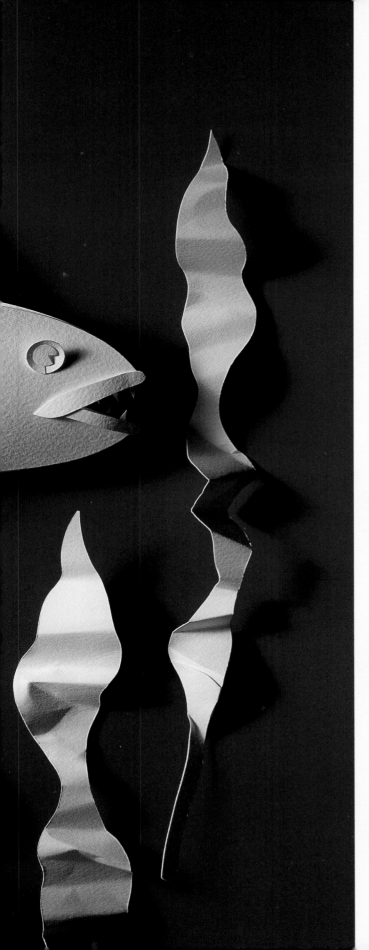

FISH

~

EQUIPMENT & MATERIALS

A3 (11³/4 x 16¹/2 in) white paper – two sheets
Scissors • Pencil
Soft eraser • PVA glue
30 cm (1 ft) rule
Small pieces of corrugated card
Clear adhesive tape

Finished size: 33 cm (13 in) approx.

F ish are a wonderful subject for paper sculpture because they have a simple body shape
and their heads, tails, fins and scales provide
an opportunity for so many decorative possibilities. When you have learned the basic techniques
you can vary the proportions of your fish.

BODY AND MOUTH

Start with an A3 (11³/4 x
16¹/2 in) sheet of white paper
and draw your chosen body
shape. This can be rounded
or sharp at both ends, thin or
fat across the body, but must
be drawn as long as the paper
will allow. Cut out the body
shape, keeping the waste
paper for later. Draw a 'V' at
one end (usually the fatter
one) and cut this out too,
making a mouth.

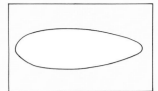

Draw body and cut out

Cut out the mouth

HEAD

Draw and cut out a second head shape, using your original as a pattern. This time join the top and bottom of the head with a curved line to form the gill cover. Curve the head and body gently over the edge of a table, remembering to keep all pencil lines on the reverse of the fish. Put a tiny touch of glue at the two ends of the fish's mouth and fasten the two heads together at these points. Glue two small pieces of corrugated card under the gill cover to hold it away from the body.

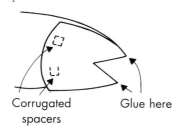

Corrugated spacers   Glue here

BODY SUPPORT

Make a cylinder about two thirds of the length of the body and 2 x 3 cm ($^3/4$ x $1^1/4$ in) diameter, depending on how wide your fish is. Turn the fish over and then glue the cylinder on to the reverse (concave) side, leaving room at the tail-end for attaching a tail. This cylinder supports the body in the centre, keeping it curved.

Glue cylinder on concave side of body

TAIL

You will need a square or oblong piece of paper for the tail. Fan-fold and wrap the base with clear adhesive tape. Cut and decorate the tail if desired before sticking it in place on the reverse (concave) side of the fish with clear adhesive tape.

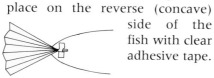

Fanfold the tail and secure with sticky tape

FINS

Cut four triangles, by cutting off the four corners of the scrap paper you saved, and fan-fold these from their leading edge.

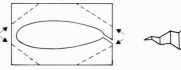

Cut fins from scrap paper   Fanfold fins

The dorsal fin on the back of the fish should be the largest and the other three are arranged on the body as shown in the photographs. Check that the rays of each fin are perpendicular to the fish's body and not horizontal! Stick each fin into place on the reverse side of the body by putting PVA on the very ends 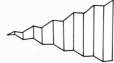 Glue fins on of the fan-folds and secure on each side with two pieces of clear adhesive tape.

Draw and cut out the side fin, which can be quite curved and flowing. The rays on this fin are cut rather than fan-folded. Bend the fin slightly with your fingers and glue it in place, angled downwards, just behind the gill cover.

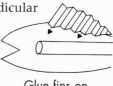

EYE

Cut out a small circle for the eye, slit to its centre, overlap the two sides of the slit and glue these together to make a shallow cone. Stick this on the head leaning it towards the nose. Cut out a pupil, smaller than the eye, and fasten this inside the eye cone with two tiny dabs of glue. The small 'V' cut out of the pupil will make the fish appear to look in different directions so try it in several positions before gluing it into place.

Eye and pupil

LIPS

Upper and lower lips are needed for your fish so look at the diagrams to see what shape they are. Notice that the top one overlaps the lower lip which is stuck into place first. Curve both lips very slightly lengthwise and only put a spot of glue at each end to hold them in position. Add sharp or rounded teeth to the mouth, or leave it toothless if you prefer!

SCALES

Scales are now added to overlap from the tail end to the gill cover. These should be of a reasonable size or the task will take forever. I make mine about 2.5 cm (1 in) diameter for a fish of A3 (11¾ x 16½ in) size. Double over some strips of paper and cut two or more scales at a time.

Bend each scale slightly in the middle (see diagram, right) before gluing it on your fish, starting at the tail. The part of each scale which bends upwards must face the tail. Trim off the scales where they overlap the body shape at the edges or use part of a scale to fill in these odd shaped areas.

Bend scales

Add scales

MAKE A 3-D FISH

Paper sculptures of different species of real fish such as perch, pike, salmon or shark can also be made using this method. You will need an accurate drawing or a good photographic reference to get the correct shapes and proportions.

It is possible to make a fully three-dimensional fish by creating a second body, a reverse of the first one, and gluing both to a supporting cylinder, sandwiching the fins and tail between the two. Make sure the cylinder is wide enough to create a good body shape. The fins and tail must be glued on to both body shapes and will help to hold them securely in place.

A variation I have enjoyed making for parties or fancy dress occasions is a three-dimensional fish large enough to fit on the head. There is no need to put an internal cylinder in this time because the head holds the two sides apart. An opening is created for the head by missing out the lower fin under the gill cover. It is best to glue an oval of thin card into this opening for extra support.

OWL

~

EQUIPMENT & MATERIALS

*A4 (8¹/4 x 11³/4 in) white or coloured paper –
two sheets*
30 cm (1 ft) Plastic rule
Pencil • Soft eraser
*A5 (5⁷/8 x 8¹/4 in) white or coloured paper –
two sheets*
Scissors • PVA glue
Cocktail stick • Compasses

Finished size: 30 cm (12 in) approx.

Models and pictures of frogs, mice, hedgehogs, pigs and owls have always been held in great affection by collectors. Probably more people have collections of these creatures than any others. I suppose it is because our folklore, stories, language and visual arts all contain numerous references to, and images of, them and we all grow up ascribing human traits to these animals.
This rhyme springs to mind:

'A wise old owl sat in an oak
And the more he sat, the less he spoke,
And the less he spoke, the more he heard,
Why can't we all be like that wise old bird.'

This wise old owl is a symbolic one, rather than a particular species, and I have used our basic shapes freely in the construction without the constraints of trying to be faithful to an actual model. This is a useful approach for any paper sculptor because the number of basic three-dimensional forms we can create from a flat sheet of paper are very limited.

It is often possible to create an effective and lifelike paper sculpture by simplifying, and perhaps even exaggerating, the forms of the subject. In this project you can see the results of such an approach, with the large, circular eye surrounds adding impact to the sculpture.

BODY AND WINGS

Three tapered cylinders are used for the owl's body and wings, and these need to be made first. Measure 5.5 cm (2¹/₈ in) in from both lower cor-

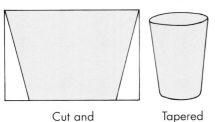

Cut and curl paper

Tapered cylinder

Cut and curl

Cut off ¹/₂ in (1cm) from top

ners of an A4 (8¹/₄ x 11³/₄ in) sheet, Houses way round (landscape), and draw two lines to form these marks with the two top corners. Do the same with two A5 (5⁷/₈ x 8¹/₄ in) sheets but this time the distance from the corners is 3 cm (1¹/₈ in) and the paper needs to be Flats way (portrait). Cut away the six triangles.

Starting with the largest trimmed sheet, put it Flats way round (portrait) and then curl it over the edge of a table, exactly as you would do with a rectangle of paper when making a cylinder. Once the piece is curled, roll it up in the palms of your hands. This makes gluing easier by removing some of the paper's springiness. Curl the two trimmed A5 (5⁷/₈ x 8¹/₄ in) sheets in the same way, this time Houses way round (landscape). Make up the three tapered cylinders, gluing and overlapping the edges by about 1 cm (¹/₂ in). Put the glue on the edge which overlaps.

Squash and join the cylinders

Once the glue is thoroughly dry, turn each one until the join is at the back, resting on the table, and gently squash flat, allowing each to pop up again with the springiness of the paper. This will create two slight folds, one at each side of the rolls. End on, the paper will no longer be a cylinder but a simple leaf-shape.

Trim 2.5 cm (1 in) off the wider ends of the thinner wing shapes. Glue them on to the body, one at a time, 1 cm (¹/₂ in) up from the base.

HEAD AND EYE SURROUND

A strip 10 cm (4 in) wide and the length of an A4 (8¹/₄ x 11³/₄ in) sheet is needed next for the head and eyes. Fold in half Flats way round (portrait) and cut into two along the fold. Fold one piece in half again, the same way, short edge to short edge. This is for the frill of feathers which surrounds both eyes. You can cut these freehand or draw them with compasses first if you wish, but do make sure they are joined together by at least 1 cm (¹/₂ in) at the centre of the folded edge. The circle for the eye-surrounds should be as big as you can make it on the folded paper.

Once the eyes are cut out, deal with the other piece which will form the head. Put a faint mark in the centre of one short edge and draw two lines from this to the two opposite corners. Cut away the two small triangles and curl the large one remaining, Flats way (portrait), over the edge of a table. Bend the pointed end to form a beak (see diagrams, right) before you glue the wide end of the triangular head inside the back of the body section, overlapping the two by about 1 cm (¹/₂ in). Leaving the bent tip of the beak free, put a little glue on to the place where it touches the body section at the front and stick it down, holding it in position until the glue sets.

Keeping the eye surrounds together, frill their outer edge to create a feathery effect before stroking each side with the fingers, to curve it slightly. This must be done while you are holding the fold so that they curve outwards from it. Open the eye surrounds and position them as shown in the diagram so that the top of the head and the beak can both be seen.

A touch of glue on both, on their reverse sides where they touch the body, will fasten them in position, finishing the basic construction.

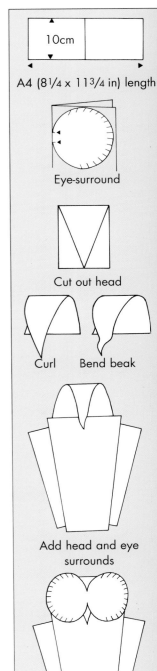

A4 (8¹/₄ x 11³/₄ in) length

Eye-surround

Cut out head

Curl   Bend beak

Add head and eye surrounds

EYES

Our owl's eyes differ from those described else-where in the book in that the integral pupil is created by scoring, rather than by adding a separate piece of paper. Draw a circle with compasses set at 2.5 cm (1 in) radius and add another circle inside it 1 cm ($\frac{1}{2}$ in) radius. Repeat for the second eye, then cut both out. Score round the inner circle with a craft knife, being careful not to cut through the paper and especially careful of your fingers, always keeping them as far away from the blade as you can. Cut a slit to the centre of each eye with scissors then gently overlap the two sides of the slit until you can pop up the centre scored section into a cone shape.

If you have completed this correctly, the cone will be standing proud inside the dish of the eye and your scoreline will be on the reverse side. Secure the overlaps on both the eyes with a spot of glue, checking that the two cones are the same height. Try the eyes in place on their feathery surrounds, then put PVA along each scoreline on the reverse sides before sticking them back in this position. I usually have the join on the eyes facing outwards at 45°.

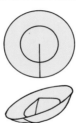

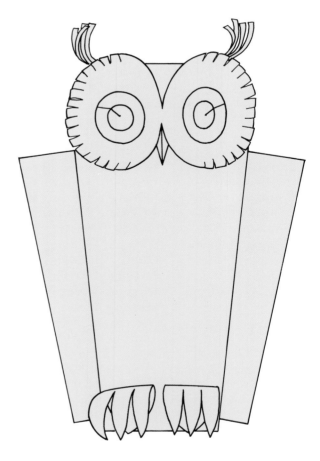

EARS

Frill two small strips of paper halfway along their length before curling the ends to make two ear tufts for the owl, then glue the plain ends inside the top of the head.

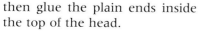
Ear tufts

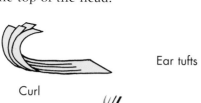
Curl

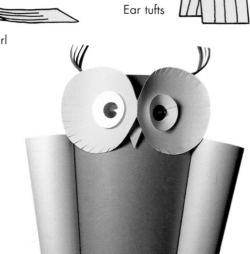

FEET

On a fold of paper cut out both feet. These are shaped like the head of a three-pronged fork. I will leave you to decide what size to make them. As with all our project work, if they prove to be too small cut two more from a larger scrap of paper. Experience is the best teacher here and, fortunately, paper is still cheap enough to allow us some trial and error in our work. Curl the feet with scissors or fingers and stick them on to the body so that the front three toes are level with its base.

Cut out the feet

Curl

TAIL

A tail is needed to finish off the back of the owl and this piece also doubles as a stand. Cut out a triangle of paper with two long sides and one short side. Curl the short side with scissors then glue its opposite point to the base of the owl at the back. Fasten it so that the tail and feet will support the owl. If you wish, you can frill the end of the tail in the same way as you did the eye surrounds.

Curl

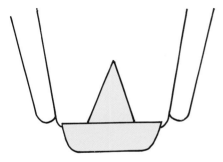

Glue tail in position

OPTIONS

Coloured papers will obviously enhance this model as you can see from the photographs. With white paper you will achieve a more sculptural effect. I prefer a plain finish to the body and wings but it is possible to add simple feathers to both areas.

If you wish to display your owl against a background, make a paper branch for him to sit on, or, as an alternative for the colour version, several owls would look splendid perching on a real branch.

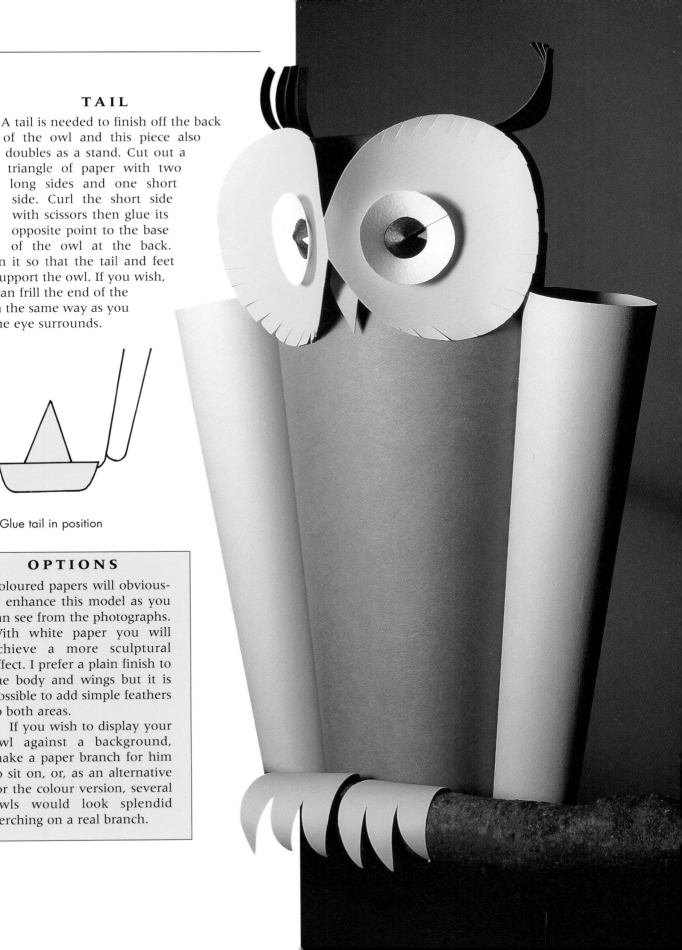

HOUSE WITH A CHIMNEY

(STRIP CONSTRUCTION)

EQUIPMENT & MATERIALS

A2 (16¹/2 x 23³/8 in) white paper – two sheets
Scissors • Small craft knife
30 cm (1 ft) Plastic rule
Steel rule • Cutting mat
PVA glue • Cocktail stick
Pencil • Soft eraser • Set square

Finished size: 23 cm (9 in) approx.

In paper sculpture repeats of a small unit, or module, always looks effective. A paper strip, scored down the centre of its width and bent to an 'L' shape is a very useful modular unit. As well as providing tabs when cut into small pieces, it gives a strong girder-like shape, ideal for constructing space frames, buildings, scaffolding and monuments such as the Eiffel Tower. It can also be used to make abstract constructions.

MAKING STRIPS

It is essential to use a strip of the correct width and weight of paper for the job in mind. I usually score strips down the centre with a craft knife and steel rule before folding them. Younger children can make do by bending half the strip at right angles along its length over the sharp edge of a desk or table, or upwards, similarly, against a rule held at half width. Make plenty of strips, all identical, before you start building with them.

Scored strip

SPACE FRAME

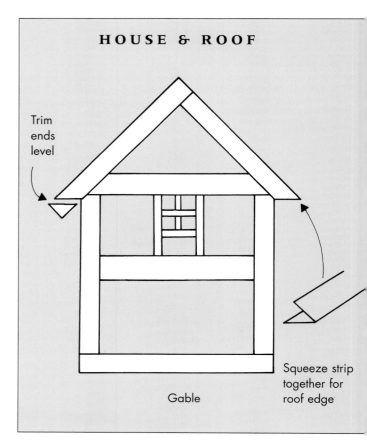

HOUSE & ROOF

Trim ends level

Gable

Squeeze strip together for roof edge

To make a simple space frame for a house, begin with the base. Cut a corner off a rectangle of card and you have a makeshift set square to check that all corners are glued at right angles, or use the real McCoy from a geometry set. You will require two sets of strips (eight altogether) to form your square or oblong base and matching top. Glue the four base strips together with their 'L' shape facing inwards, checking that each corner is a true right angle with your set square. Construct the top in the same way.

When these two pieces are dry, glue on four identical, vertical strips, one inside each corner of the base, again checking that they are perfectly upright with the set square. The top is now glued on to these verticals with the 'L' shape the opposite way round to the base and your space frame is ready for modification into a house.

45°

Card set square

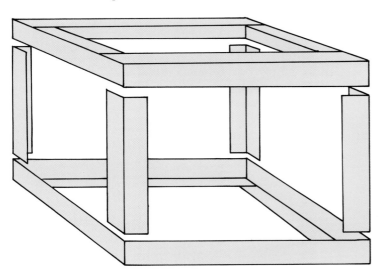

Constructing the space frame

Halls, castles, churches, cathedrals and other more ambitious architectural monuments can all be built in a similar way to this house.

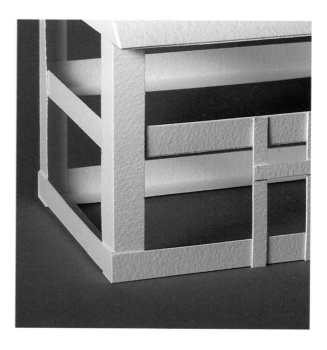

Cut a ridge and two roof edge strips the same length as the long side of the house. Two long strips are also needed to form the gables of the roof. These gable strips are cut halfway through the 'L' shape in the centre of the strip. Overlap and glue them at this point at your chosen angle for the gable.

Look carefully at the diagrams and photographs to understand how to fit the gable and roof structure on to the original space frame. Note that the two gables must be identical and allow a small overlap at each end for attaching the edge strips of the roof once the gables are trimmed as shown. Join the gables on to your space frame, trim to length parallel to your work-surface, then add the ridge and the roof edges.

A second storey can be created by adding strips halfway between the ground floor and the roof. Both ground floor and second floor can now be filled in with sheets of paper if you wish. Hold these in position by gluing them to the inner leg of the 'L' shaped strips. If you plan to add

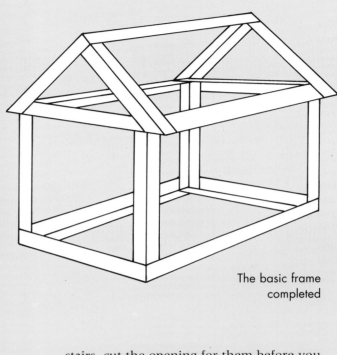

The basic frame completed

stairs, cut the opening for them before you glue in the second storey floor.

TO MAKE THE CHIMNEY

Make a chimney using the technique for constructing cuboids given in Project 2. Cut triangles out of opposite sides of the chimney base to fit the roof angle at the ridge and use four small pieces of 'L' strip as tabs to attach this item to the roof. Stick on a square top, slightly larger than the stack, and make one or more small cylinders for chimneys. Apply glue neatly to their edges with a cocktail stick, place in position and leave until the glue sets.

Once the basic house is completed, doors, windows and exterior details such as guttering can be added. If you decide not to fill in the walls, leaving the space frame construction, then rooms, stairs,

furniture and interior decor can make the whole piece even more sculpturally interesting.

I usually attach my doors and windows by using single, unfolded strips to form their surrounding supporting timbers, joining these to the floors or sides of the building. This gives a similar effect to a timber-framed house and can be followed through by adding various decorative, diagonal and curved mouldings at this stage of construction.

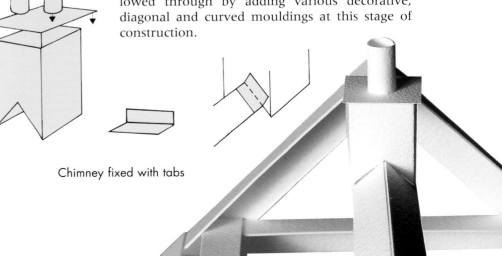

Chimney fixed with tabs

TO MAKE ARCHES

Saxon (rounded) and Norman (pointed) arches are easily made using the strip method. Saxon arches need the 'L' strip cut halfway through at small regular intervals over the intended curved part of the strip's length. A gentle bend made with the fingers will then round this section.
Complete the arch by adding a curved piece of paper, half the width of the strip, to hold the small, cut 'bricks' in place.

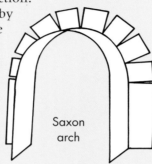

Saxon arch

A Norman arch needs only a central cut halfway through the 'L' strip. Fold or score lightly and crease at this point, then curve each side to form a pointed arch.
Complete by overlapping two small strips of paper to fill in the open 'V' at the top and trim these to a point when the glue is dry. Both arches will need a suitable length of 'L' strip to form their bases.

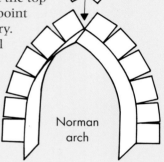

Norman arch

GIRDERS

Strip construction is a very exciting way of building in paper because it allows you to see the sculpture develop. Because the 'L' strips look like girders they are especially effective when used for architectural features such as bridges, towers, building site constructions and pylons.

The 'L' strips can be modified and strengthened by gluing two or more together in different ways to give other girder shapes (see diagrams).

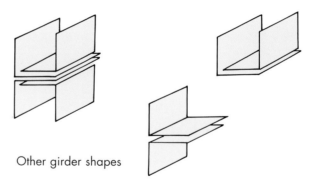

Other girder shapes

CUBOIDS & CYLINDERS

Combining cuboids and cylinders with our 'L' strips will make even more exciting constructions possible.

If you make a street of buildings or, even more ambitiously, tackle a whole town then keep all the individual buildings as near as possible to the same scale, so they fit in well visually, one with the other. Teachers and children in school could use a maths lesson to work out an accurate scale on graph paper. Simple scale drawings with both side and end elevations, and a plan – the sort of thing an architect might produce – are also tremendously useful if you want to make a detailed model of a particular building.

Working non-stop for a day at a recent school workshop on historic French buildings we managed to create a model of the Eiffel Tower in thin card and paper, which reached from the classroom floor to its ceiling: a typical example of the exciting possibilities this method of construction offers to the paper sculptor.

PROJECT 9

LEAVES

EQUIPMENT & MATERIALS

A3 (11³/4 x 16¹/2 in) white or coloured papers
Scissors • Small craft knife
Cutting mat
PVA glue • Cocktail sticks
Pencil • Soft eraser

Finished size: life size approx.

Leaves and flowers are traditional paper sculpture decorations. Both are normally used in bas-

relief designs fastened to a suitable background. When sculptured in white paper on a coloured background, with side-lighting, the results can look very dramatic but are achieved by the simplest of means. Leaves are often used as borders and repeat motifs with lettering. Coloured paper can also be used to great effect with even the simplest of leaf shapes.

SIMPLE LEAVES

Cut out a simple leaf shape and score from point to point. Crease the scoreline then curve the whole leaf widthwise over the edge of a table making sure that the scoreline is on the underside. This will give a simple laurel-type leaf which is very effective in border decorations or garlands with several grouped together. Complicated borders to leaves are

Cut

Score

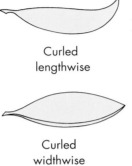

Curve

Add edges after basic shape

best added after the basic shape has been cut out and creased.

Leaves can also be shaped by gently curving opposite ends lengthwise or by curling the blade across its width. Even a slight bend to the leaf point will give a sculptural effect when stuck down. These variations of treatment can be used on many types of leaves. As with all paper sculpture, any three-dimensional quality added to your leaves will make them more convincing. I generally use scored and shaped strips of paper of different widths for longer leaf stalks and twigs. Remember that by scoring and creasing you will reduce the width of these strips.

Curled lengthwise

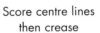

Curled widthwise

HOLLY

Holly leaves can be made more sculptural by scoring to the side points as well as along the central vein of the leaf. Crease all of these scorelines before turning the leaf over and scoring between the points. Push gently from the pointed end of the leaf once the creasing is complete to create a spiky quality.

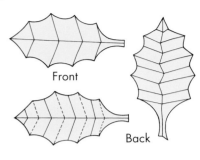

Front

Back

Berry

Add berries by cutting to the centre of small circles, then overlapping and gluing the cut edges to make shallow cones. Always glue the shallow cones with the open side upwards for the best effect. Dark green holly with red berries looks particularly splendid when made in this way for Christmas decorations.

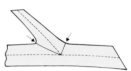

Score centre lines then crease

Turn over and score joins

Holly twigs need scoring down their centreline and to the end of each stalk (see diagrams).

Crease these scorelines then turn the twig over, scoring and creasing to each side of the stalks. Branches and twigs are almost always fastened into place before leaves are added.

IDEAS FOR LEAVES

Exotic leaves such as palms and yuccas tend to grow spirally up the stem. Re-create this growth pattern by winding a long strip of leaves round a central cylinder, starting at the top and carefully gluing each turn as you travel downwards.

Younger children often enjoy creating imaginary leaves using each of the five paper sculpture techniques in turn. This kind of exploration of a subject usually produces weird, wonderful and surprising results.

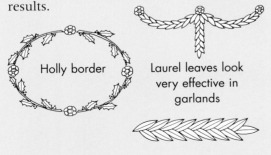

Holly border

Laurel leaves look very effective in garlands

TWIGS AND BRANCHES

Twigs and branches to support the leaves can be textured in a number of ways. You can make additions to a basic shape, such as rough strips glued round a branch to imitate Birch bark, or the strips can be curved to represent blemishes on smoother trunks such as Ash or Rowan, or they can be crumpled tightly before teasing apart for trees with rough, textured bark such as Oak and Sweet Chestnut.

FLOWERS

EQUIPMENT & MATERIALS

A3 (11³/4 x 16¹/2 in) white paper
A4 (8¹/4 x 11³/4 in) white paper
Scissors • Small craft knife
30 cm (1 ft) Plastic rule
Cutting mat
Pencil • Soft eraser
PVA glue • Cocktail sticks
Compasses
A4 (8¹/4 x 11³/4 in) photocopying paper –
two sheets
Tracing paper

Finished size: life size approx.

These flower forms will look very attractive made in white or coloured paper. Both the daffodils and lilies can be displayed either in a vase or fastened to a background, while the waterlily is designed to fit into bas-relief arrangements with leaves.

In white paper the waterlily can double as a Christmas rose and I have often used it in this guise with holly leaves, twigs and berries for exhibitions at Christmas time.

WATERLILY

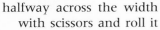

Cut three

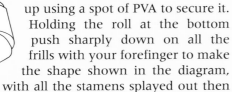

Curl ends

We will begin with the waterlily which is the easiest of the three flowers. Cut three paper strips whose length is approximately three times their width. Holding these tightly together, round off both ends with scissors. Now curl all the rounded ends of the strips with scissors, or by rolling them round a pencil, leaving the middle third of each one flat. Stick two of the curled strips together so the petals touch at each end or, for those with a mathematical turn of mind, crossed at 120° to each other. This just leaves room for the third strip, which is glued into this space.

Two petals touching

Add third petal

Lily stamens

To complete this flower cut a strip the same width and half the length of the petals, frill this finely halfway across the width with scissors and roll it up using a spot of PVA to secure it. Holding the roll at the bottom push sharply down on all the frills with your forefinger to make the shape shown in the diagram, with all the stamens splayed out then meeting again in the centre.

This is another of those occasions when I wish I could show you personally. Even the best description and competent illustrations can sometimes leave a reader feeling completely mystified as to the process involved. Looking at the photograph and diagrams of our waterlily might help but, failing this, curl, crush or pleat the stamens in any way you wish – they

will still look alright. Place a blob of PVA into the centre of the flower and push the rolled end of the stamens into this. Put your flowers to one side and allow this glue to dry thoroughly before using them in an arrangement.

DAFFODIL PETALS

Cut centre

Score both sides

Photocopy and trace the pattern for the daffodil flowerhead and cut this piece out. On one side make three scorelines running across the centre from petal tip to petal tip.

These scorelines must bisect the petals accurately, so make a tiny mark with a hard pencil on the tip of each if you need a guide. Crease each scoreline then turn the flowerhead over and score three more lines, this time in between the petals. Complete the creasing then pinch the petals until they form a good daffodil shape.

TRUMPET

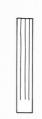

Daffodil stamens

Make the trumpet by tracing the circle segment given on to paper, cutting it out and making this into a cone. Pinch the point in one hand then twist one edge over the other into a cone shape to relax the paper before you glue the two edges together, keeping the overlap as small as you can. Cut a wavy edge or frill the open end of the trumpet if you want it to look even more authentic. This is easier to do before constructing the cone.

Snip four little slits into the pointed base of the flower petals, put a little PVA on the end of the cone and push it into the cut centre of the petals. Leave to dry while you cut three or four fine strips in a scrap of paper the same length as the trumpet, for stamens and anthers. Curl the free ends of the anthers and squeeze them together at their base before applying a spot of glue to it and pushing them into the bottom of the trumpet.

BUD COVER

In a real daffodil there is a papery cover which protects the bud and its remains can normally be seen behind the flowerhead when this is open. Our paper equivalent will be a narrow cone which will join the stalk on to the bloom. Make the cover in the same way as you did the trumpet, but use thin typing or photocopying paper as this is easier to manipulate into such a narrow shape. Hold a pencil inside the cone, on the join, while the glue dries. Cut four equidistant slits around the open end and then trim about 4 mm ($^5/_{16}$ in) from the point so you will be able to push the stalk inside. Spread the tabs you have created at the open end and use them to fasten the cone centrally on to the back of the bloom.

STALK

Roll an A4 ($8^1/_4$ x $11^3/_4$ in) sheet of thin photocopying or typing paper as tightly as you can for the flower stalk, sticking the loose end down in the centre. If you have rolled it correctly from one corner to the other diagonally, the end of the paper should be in this central position. Trim off both ends until the roll is firm to the touch, spread a little glue on one end and push this into the hole in the cone-shaped bud cover. Stand the flower upright in a jar to avoid undue pressure on the bloom while the glue dries.

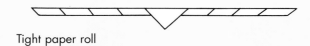

Tight paper roll

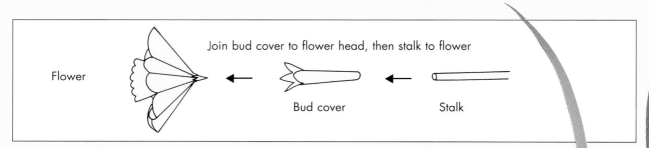

Flower

Join bud cover to flower head, then stalk to flower

Bud cover   Stalk

LEAVES

Two thin strips, pointed at one end, are needed for the leaves. Cut them the length of the flower and stalk combined. Score from top to bottom, beginning at the point, then crease this scoreline from the wide end. A little glue inside the base of each leaf will suffice to attach them to the bottom of the stalk, one above the other, and on opposite sides. If you wish you can bend the tip of one leaf over, reversing this part of its scoreline. Finish your daffodil by gently pulling the head downwards to give the correct angle of bloom to stalk.

Daffodil leaf

LILY

Once you have made the lily blossom, the process of preparing the pieces and putting them together is identical to the daffodil; only sizes and shapes will differ.

Trace and cut out the shape for the bloom and form this into a cone. You will already have had practise with cones if you made a daffodil – if not, a few trial runs with rough paper are an invaluable experience. I have allowed an overlap of one whole petal in the lily head, so apply glue to this overlapping petal and stick it on top of its adjacent twin once you have formed a good cone shape. This gives the flower its correct complement of five petals. Once the doubled petal has dried, curl it and the remaining four petals outwards to give your bloom the proper shape. Petals can be curled with scissors, round a pencil, or bent carefully with the fingers. Your choice of technique will depend not only on your expertise, but also on the thickness of paper used for the flower.

Lily pattern

STEM

Roll a stem the same way as for the daffodil but cut four tiny slits in one end when gluing and trimming is complete. Apply glue to the outside of the tabs once you have spread them a little, also putting some on to the stem just below them. Cut off the point of the flower cone to make a hole just big enough for the stem and push it through the flowerhead until the sticky tabs are resting right in the neck of the flower. Inserting a pencil to hold them there while the glue dries is a good idea.

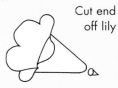
Cut end off lily

LEAVES & STAMENS

Cut out three leaves, making them shorter and wider than the daffodils and tapering them at both ends. Score and crease in the usual way down the centre of each one, then glue its base on to the stalk. A minimum of glue is needed here or the paper will go soggy and the resulting join look messy. Space the three leaves at equal intervals up the stem, the first one near the base of the flower. Cut a group of stamens, curl one end and glue the other into the throat of the lily.

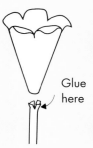
Glue here

Insert stem from wide end of bloom

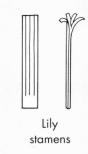
Lily stamens

DISPLAYS WITH DAFFODILS

These instructions can be adapted to make miniature and giant versions of these flowers. A group of five year olds I taught some years ago made daffodils as tall as themselves, in full colour, and these made a truly memorable spring display. Garden canes were substituted for the paper stems and, once the flowerheads had been fixed in place, strips of crêpe paper were wrapped tightly and diagonally round them as a cover. A touch of clear adhesive tape secured the loose end.

We planted our giant daffodils in large pots filled with sand, which were grouped in the school foyer, where they lasted well for three months and gave a great deal of pleasure.

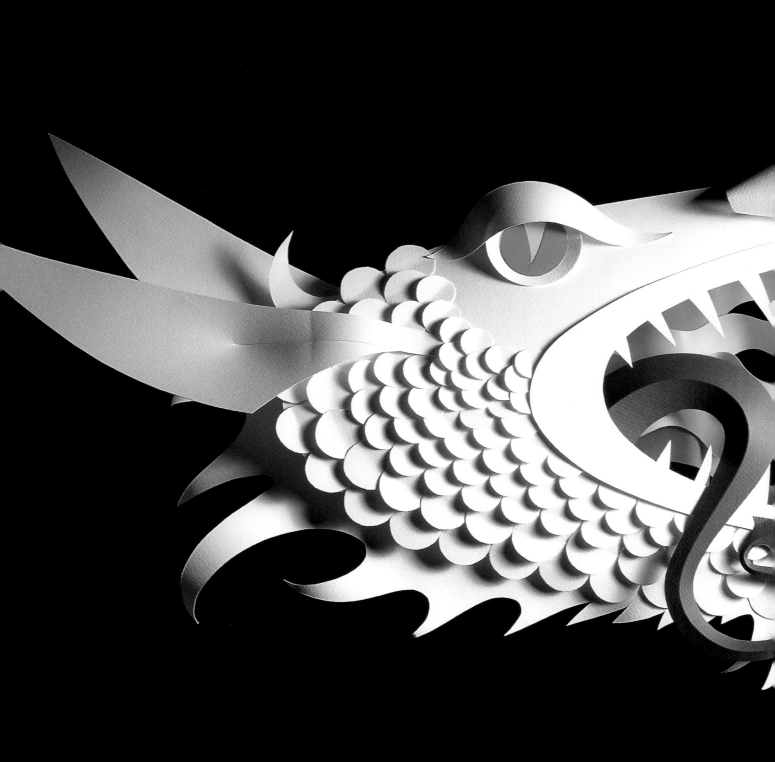

FIERY DRAGON'S HEAD

~

EQUIPMENT & MATERIALS

A3 (11³/4 x 16¹/2 in) white paper – three sheets
Pencil • Soft eraser
Scissors • Small craft knife
Cutting mat
PVA glue • Cocktail sticks
A4 (8¹/4 x 11³/4 in) red paper (optional)
A5 (5⁷/8 x 8¹/4 in) green paper (optional)
A4 (8¹/4 x 11³/4 in) orange paper (optional)
A4 (8¹/4 x 11³/4 in) yellow paper (optional
A5 (5⁷/8 x 8¹/4 in) black paper (optional)

Finished size: 760 cm (30 in) approx.

Dragons have always captured the imagination and feature in folklore the world over, from Japan and China to England and Wales.

This bas-relief dragon's head has a simple construction which nevertheless looks very dramatic when all the details such as eyes, nostrils, ears, scales, teeth and fire have been added.

The techniques contained in this project can be easily adapted for you to create all kinds of bird, animal and human heads. Portraits from science fiction, fantasy, myth and magic can also be treated in the same way and look wonderful as multiple displays.

HEAD

A3 (11³/4 x 16¹/2 in) paper is used for this head because it allows all details, particularly the scales, to be of a reasonable size for easy handling and construction.

Draw head

Cut out

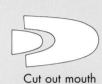

Cut out mouth

Place your paper Houses way round (landscape) and draw a rounded 'V' or 'U' shape on it. This drawn curve should begin top left, touch centre right and end in the bottom left hand corner. Cut round your line, neatening it as necessary, saving the scrap pieces for later. Draw a similar, but smaller, shape for the mouth of your dragon, making the mouth central on the one remaining straight edge (see diagrams), and then cutting it out.

Turn the head over, pencil marks underneath, and curve slightly over the edge of a table, keeping the paper Houses way round (landscape). Make a small cylinder, to support the centre of the head, and glue this on the reverse, concave side. Its ends should be facing the back of the head and the centre of the mouth. If you wish, the head can then be attached to a coloured backing sheet at this stage, fastening it by the cylinder and two tabs, one on each jaw. Having the sculpture on a background certainly makes for easier handling and display.

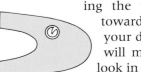

Curve and add cylinder

EYE

Cut two circles of appropriate diameters for the eye and pupil. Cut the eye disc to its centre and overlap and glue the two edges to make a shallow cone. Snip a small 'V' out of the pupil before sticking this inside the eye with a couple of small blobs of PVA on its edges.

Make the eye

Try the eye in place on the head and make a small pencil mark where it looks best before gluing it down, keeping the tilt of the shallow cone towards the nose or lower jaw of your dragon. The 'V' in the pupil will make the dragon appear to look in the direction this is placed.

EARS

Next you will need a long rectangle of paper folded in half Houses way round (landscape) to cut the ears from. Your dragon's ears can be any shape within this oblong but do keep them of a reasonable length. Draw directly on one side of the paper, or round a pattern you have made, and cut both ears out together. Cutting round the ears on the 'open' side first then the folded side

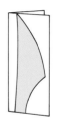

Cut out the ears

will prevent the shapes from slipping.

Keeping the two ears together, make a slit, from the centre base of the shapes to halfway up the ears. One edge of this slit is then pulled and glued over the other to create a hollow and a bend in each ear. Remember to do this the opposite way round to the second ear. Trim the base of the front ear, either rounding it off or cutting a spiky finish. There is no need to trim the rear one as its base will not be seen.

Stick the front ear in place. The rear one can be either fastened onto the reverse side of the head or to the background if you have one. Offset the ears slightly so you can see both of them.

Slit and overlap ears

EYELID

Once the ears are in place, glue the dragon's eyelid over the top of the eye at an angle to give it a fierce rather than a friendly look. Cut a simple curve above the straight edge of a small length of paper to create the eyebrow. Because it curves over the top of the eye, make sure you cut this piece long enough to be able to glue each end down to secure it.

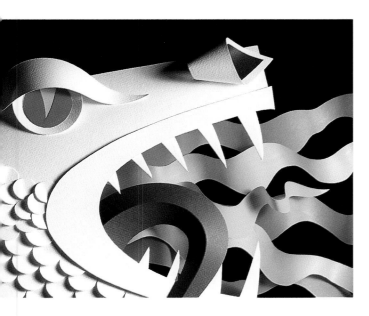

NOSTRIL

Only one nostril is needed for the dragon and this is created by crossing a strip of paper over itself to make a cone shape and by using a spot of glue to fix it where the ends cross. These ends are then trimmed to a point. Position it with the pointed side facing the front of the dragon's nose.

Nostril strip

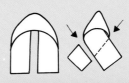

Cross over strip for nostrils and trim

TEETH

Add the teeth next, cutting them in pairs from a folded strip of paper, scoring and creasing each one before gluing it inside the mouth. Only put glue on one side of the scoreline so the teeth keep their three-dimensional quality inside the dragon's mouth.

Score teeth

TONGUE

A slightly 'S' shaped tongue looks good, especially if it has a barbed end. Be sure you score and crease it in the same way as you did the teeth before fixing it inside the mouth. Remember that scoring and creasing increase the curve of the tongue.

FIRE

All dragons breathe fire and smoke and ours is no exception to the rule. Cut out the fire with uneven, wavy lines along the edges of each individual flame. Attach the fiery shapes inside the mouth behind the tongue or on to the background, again behind the tongue and inside the dragon's mouth.

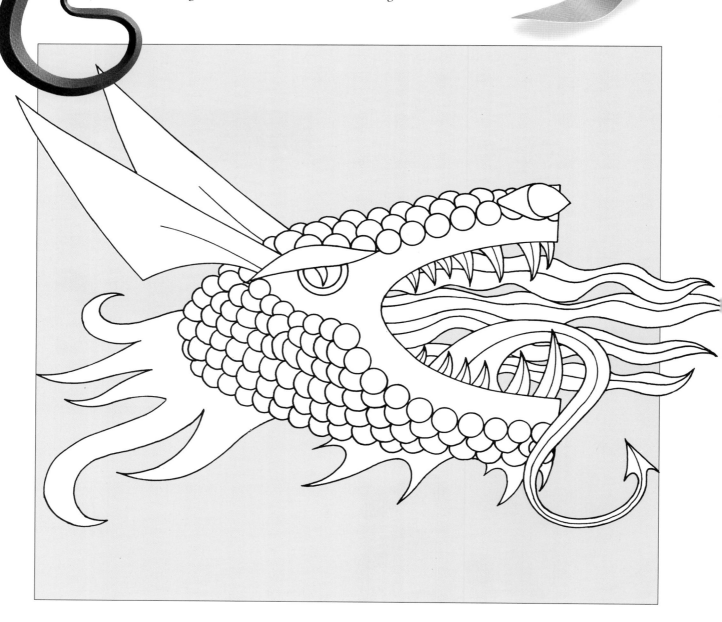

SCALES

Add scales from the back of the head, working forwards and overlapping as you go. Make the scales by cutting suitably sized circles, two at a time, from doubled over strips of paper. Each scale is then bent slightly at its centre so that it can be glued down at its front end. Tip up the scales as you glue them to the head, overlapping them like tiles on a roof. I like to leave the areas around the dragon's lips and eye free of scales to draw attention to these features and for added textural interest.

A few spiky pieces of bent and curled paper at the chin, the back of the head and below the ears complete our fiery dragon's head.

As you can see, coloured papers for the pupil, tongue and fire make striking additions and act as a foil to the white paper.

FATHER CHRISTMAS

~

EQUIPMENT & MATERIALS

A3 (11³/4 x 16¹/2 in) red paper
A3 (11³/4 x 16¹/2 in) white paper
A2 (16¹/2 x 23³/8 in) black paper
A5 (5⁷/8 x 8¹/4 in) pink paper
Pencil • Soft eraser
Compasses • Scissors
30 cm (1 ft) Plastic rule
PVA glue • Cocktail sticks

Finished size: 41 cm (16 in) approx.

This model of Father Christmas is not only fun to create but makes a splendid decoration for the house or the dining table during Christmastide.

Several years ago I made four of the same sculptures, 6 m (20 ft) high, as decorations for the International Show Jumping Championships at Olympia in London, and these giant models were just as appealing despite their great size.

BASIC SHAPE

Draw as large a quarter segment of a circle as you can with compasses on red A3 (11³/4 x 16¹/2 in) paper and cut this out, retaining the spare piece for the arms. Curl the segment over a sharp table edge as you would a cylinder but change the

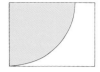

Cut segment
from paper

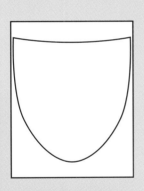

Make
cone

movement slightly so you retain the point, which should face towards you, in position on the table. Curl the circumference of the shape well to relax it and make it easier to form into a cone. Pinch the point slightly in one hand while the other winds the paper, one edge inside the other, as tightly as possible, into a cone. Try to keep the edge at the open end level as you do this. The paper should now form a cone shape, ready for gluing along to the inside of the overlapping edge.

The overlap needs to be about 2 cm ($^3/4$ in) at the open end or it will be difficult to form a point because the overlapping edge tapers towards the tip of the cone. Hold the cone in front of you with the glued edge resting on the table. Overlap the free edge, at the same time making sure that the two parts of the circumference level up then, using your hand with a finger extended, or a pencil, reach up inside and hold the join in place until the glue sets.

It is difficult to make cones because the paper often cockles on the join and creates an unwanted opening at the point. Practice makes perfect here and it is a good idea for beginners to try producing several cones in rough paper until they get the hang of the process.

TO MAKE THE FACE

Cut a face shape (see diagrams) from a rectangle of pink paper 7 x 6.5 cm (2¾ x 2½ in). It may be easier to cut out a pattern from folded scrap paper first, check the size and shape, and then draw round this on to the pink paper before cutting out the finished face. Note that the top of the face is slightly curved downwards, from the centre to the edges.

Cut face shape

Cut out two oval eyes from a fold of white paper and a round nose from a scrap of red. Colour in the black pupils with a felt tip pen leaving a spot of white to give the illusion of a reflection in them. The pupils may be top or bottom, left or right – each option creating a different expression to the face. Position the eyes and nose, leaving room for the eyebrows at the top and the moustache lower down, then stick them down with a spot of glue on each piece.

Father Christmas's moustache is cut from a folded strip and can be curly, spiralled, bushy or straight, or any other style and size you choose. Experiment with several moustaches then glue on the one which suits best under the nose. Give it a lively curl by bending the ends slightly before or after gluing.

Lift the moustache once the glue is dry and colour in a black segment underneath. Draw a line below this segment to create the lower lip and complete the mouth. Finish off the face with eyebrows made from a small folded scrap of paper. Match them to the moustache, bend them up in the middle then stick them on, using a touch of glue on each end.

Complete face

Fold

Cut
moustache

HAIR & BEARD

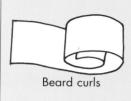

Beard curls

Glue curls to back of face

Make lots of curled strips for Santa's hair and beard and then glue these carefully on to the back of the face, overlapping them slightly so that there are no empty gaps. Make sure they grow in the right direction as you stick them round the curve of the face. Fasten the finished face to the front of your cone, touching the base of the hat. Put your free hand up inside the cone so you can press lightly, holding the face in position while the glue dries.

POM-POM

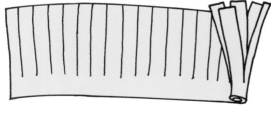

Make a pom-pom for the hat

Create a pom-pom for the hat by making lots of fine cuts along a small strip of paper, rolling it up and securing the end, before curling or spreading the cut ends to make them look fluffy. Glue the point of the hat and ease this into your pom-pom.

FUR TRIM

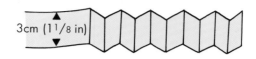

3cm (1¹/8 in)

Fanfold fur trim to hat and coat in folds of about ¹/2 in (1cm)

Next cut three strips, 3 cm (1¹/8 in) wide, from the long edge of a sheet of white A3 (11¾ x 16¹/2 in) paper. Stick two together so you have one short and one long strip. Concertina fold these strips at about 1 cm (¹/2 in) intervals then join up the ends of each one, so you have two rings. Make a generous line of glue, 1 cm (¹/2 in) above the open end of the cone, and gently push the larger of the two fan-folded rings on to it, giving a white fur-trimmed border to the edge of Father Christmas's coat. Leave this to dry thoroughly before the next step.

Draw a line round the top of the cone 10 cm (4 in) from its point and repeat the gluing process, pushing the smaller pleated ring down into the glue to form the lower edge of the conical hat.

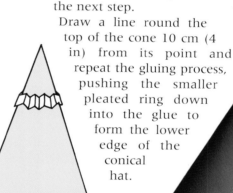

Attach fan-folded rings

ARMS

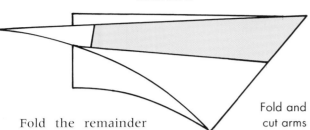

Fold and cut arms

Fold the remainder of the red paper, matching the two straight edges to create a diagonal crease. Cut the two arms together, starting about 12 cm (4¾ in) from the point of the fold and cutting where the two pieces cross at the far edge. Finally, trim off the odd side in order to level the cuffs so that they are about 3.5 cm (1³/8 in) wide.

GLOVES

Draw and cut out two mittens from a small piece of folded black paper, matching their width to that of the cuffs. Glue the mittens in position thumbs up, and add two folded strips of white paper, 3 cm (1¹/8 in) wide, to cover the join between the arm and the glove.

Two cuffs

Apply glue to the inside of the foldline, between the two arms, and stick them in place on the join of the cone with their point touching the lower edge of the hat. Later you may wish to bend one or both arms at the elbows as Father Christ-mas touches the edge of his coat, or his beard, and fix them in this position.

12cm

Stick on arms

BOOTS

You will need a piece of black paper 12 cm (4¾ in) wide, cut from the short edge of an A2 (16¹/2 x 23³/8 in) sheet for Santa's boots. Make a a simple cylinder, overlapping by a 1 cm (¹/2 in) at the back, and glue inside the cone. Put a generous line of glue round the very top edge of the cylinder then, making sure the join is at the back and matching that of the cone, slide this gently down until they touch. Keep the cone absolutely vertical while you do this or Father Christmas may look a little tipsy.

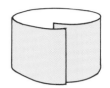

Make base cylinder

To finish off your model you may like to bend the arms and glue the hands holding his tummy, as if he were laughing, or have one glove touching his beard which will give him a surprised look. This sort of finishing touch can give your paper sculptures character and individuality.

Once the festive season is over, pop your Father Christmas into a clear plastic bag, seal it, and store him somewhere dry. You will be able to enjoy his cheerful presence for several years if he is kept in this way.

ANGEL

Images of Father Christmas and angels, pagan and Christian symbols together, abound during the festive season. Both as popular as each other, they come in all sorts of shapes, sizes and designs, and I knew that I wanted to include projects of my own versions when I planned this book. A small angel would look splendid topping your Christmas tree and the cone-shaped body should sit easily in place.

Traditional, white paper sculpture is ideal for angels but you can use suitably coloured paper for the face, hair and hands if you wish. Our version sings from a book, but raise the arms to support a cone-shaped trumpet or lower them to play a harp to give two more variations.

The whole of the Sunday School at a local Church made fifty angels one Christmastide and they looked wonderful, suspended right across the building, above the altar.

CONE BODY

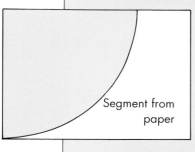

Segment from paper

Start with an A3 (11³/4 x 16¹/2 in) sheet of paper and draw as large a quarter segment of a circle on it as you can, then cut this out. If you have only ordinary compasses the size can be achieved by extending your pencil outwards as far as it will go. Make this segment into a cone, overlapping the paper at its open end by 2.5cm (1 in). If you are not sure how to form the cone read the description of this process given in the previous project on Father Christmas.

Make cone

CAPE

Make the cape by bending the two top corners of a sheet of A4 (8¹/4 x 11³/4 in) paper inwards to overlap each other. Be sure you have this houses way round (landscape) and try it for size, before sticking one corner over the other. The top aperture in the cape needs to fit loosely when it sits in place on the cone. Put a little glue inside the back of the cape to secure it to the cone body. Reduce the height of the cone by cutting 1 cm (¹/2 in) off its point.

Bend corners of paper

Glue cape at corners

Add cape and cut 1cm (¹/2 in) off cone

FACE

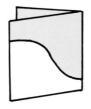

Face pattern

Draw and cut out a pattern for the face from a small, folded rectangle of paper. Open the pattern and draw around it. Cut out the head proper and put on the features while it is still flat.

◄ 13 cm (5¹/8 in) ►

Make head

Make the eyebrows and nose from scraps of paper – the eyes and a singing mouth are cut in with a sharp craft knife.

5 cm (2 in)

Curl the head, overlapping by 1 cm (¹/2 in) at the back and gluing; now glue on the back of the head level with the end of the protruding cone.

HAIR

Give your angel a coiffure next, cutting the long hair to go round the head first, bending all the middle sections in, and curling the ends outwards with scissors, or round a cocktail stick. The fringe and the top of the head is all one piece: a 7 cm (2³/4 in) circle with strips cut into it all the way round and curled with scissors. Be careful when cutting these strips because they taper from the circumference to the middle and only need to be cut halfway to the centre of the circle. A little PVA applied round the top of the head will hold this top knot in position and a finger laid gently on the hair until the glue sets is a sensible precaution.

7cm (2³/4 in)

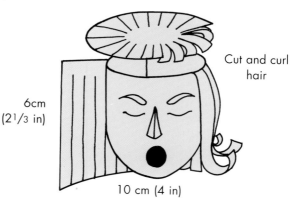

Cut and curl hair

6cm (2¹/3 in)

10 cm (4 in)

BOOK, HANDS AND SLEEVES

Book, hands and sleeves are put together as a complete unit before they are attached and this makes the positioning of the shoulders easier. Two hands are cut out of one fold of paper and a book out of another. Curve the covers of the book gently over the edge of a table or with scissors, curling downwards to give an authentic bend to the covers and attach the hands, thumbs up, to the book.

Curve the sleeves in the centre of their width over a table top or round a pencil then glue at their lower edges. Round the shoulders with scissors and cut through the whole sleeve just over 6 cm (2³/8 in) from the cuff.

Reassemble at an angle, pushing the glued upper section over the lower one, and trimming off the excess, from the elbow to the lower front edge of the cuff.

Glue the hands holding the book into the top, front edge of each sleeve by their extended wrists. Once the glue on all the joined pieces is thoroughly dry, glue the shoulders into place on the cape, bearing in mind the angle of the head.

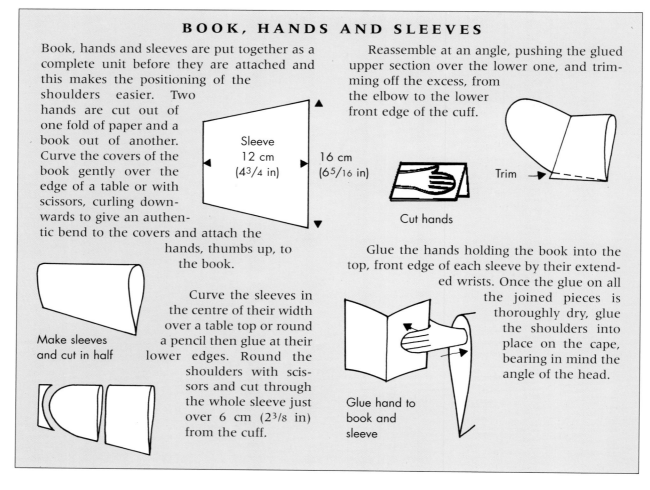

Sleeve 12 cm (4³/4 in)

16 cm (6⁵/16 in)

Cut hands

Trim →

Make sleeves and cut in half

Glue hand to book and sleeve

WINGS

Wings are made from a folded rectangle of paper and should be cut to suit the size of your angel's body (see photograph). I like to have two sections to the wings, because it makes them more decorative, but single wings are just as acceptable. Three or four cuts up from the angled base of the wings will create feathers. Trim the inner edge of the feathers to make them pointed then give each one a slight bend with the fingers.

Once you have cut out the wings, fold them parallel to the original crease, from the 1 cm (¹/2 in) mark on the shoulder. This will give you a 2 cm (³/4 in) strip to fasten them on with, the creases allowing the wings to be displayed at an angle. Apply PVA to the central strip and position the wings vertically in the middle of the angel's

back, with the rounded wing-tops approximately level with the mouth when viewed from the front. If you put your hand inside the cone you will be able to hold the wings in place while the glue sets. If you cut out the extra feathers for the top of the wings these can be attached now, sticking them down in the centre and at the edges.

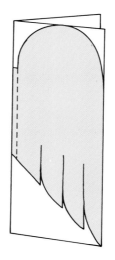

Cut out and attach the wings

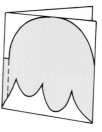

HALO

A halo for your angel is an optional extra. This symbol is usually drawn in a single line or portrayed as a fine ring of light in pictures and you may feel that a circle of paper looks awkward and wide in comparison. Cut out a ring in the flat and try it in place to judge the effect for yourself. I sometimes cut mine out of silver or gold card to give a sparkling finish to an all-white angel. Attach your halo with a touch of glue to the back of the hair, so that it frames the head.

OPTIONS

If you want to suspend your angel use a needle and cotton thread, or monofilament line, through its back, near the junction of the wings. This will allow your sculpture to slope slightly forwards and looks more natural than having it flying bolt upright.

These angels are easy to make in bigger sizes because the cone is stable and will support the rest of the pieces. If you are making a life-size version then it will need inside support with a cardboard body-cone, covered with paper.

Once you have increased the size, you may wish to increase the amount of sculptural detail. Decorative hems and cuffs and more substantial wings can be added. Large wings will need a card base to hold them rigid; white cardboard is preferable in this instance.

With a little ingenuity you could display your angel as part of a Nativity scene, with figures of Mary, Joseph, the shepherds and the three kings, all constructed on cone bases. Baby Jesus is the only variation and would need a cylindrical body to wrap the paper swaddling clothes round.

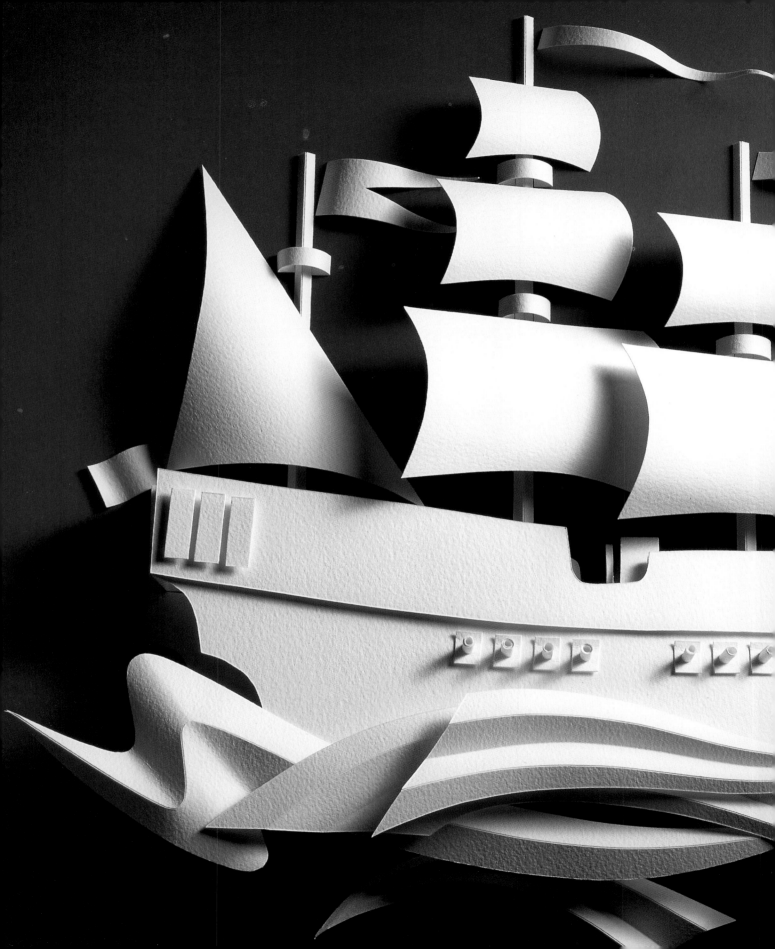

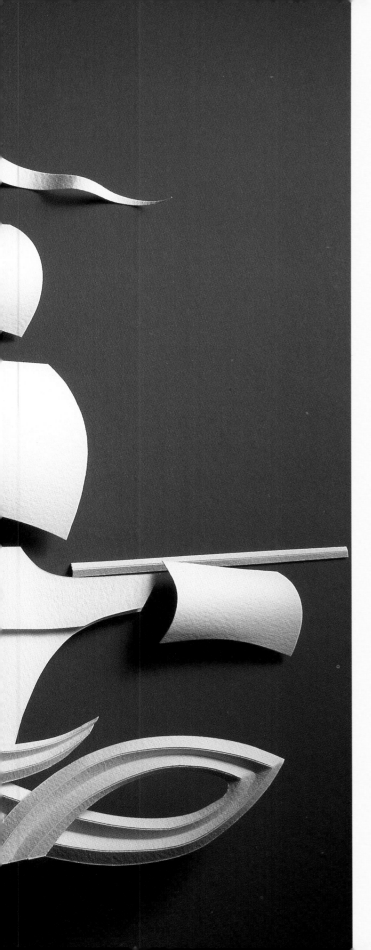

GALLEON

~≈~

EQUIPMENT & MATERIALS

A4 (8¹/4 x 11³/4 in) white paper – four sheets
Pencil • Soft eraser
Scissors • Small craft knife
Cutting mat
30 cm (1 ft) Plastic rule
Tracing paper
A2 (16¹/2 x 23³/8 in) blue paper
PVA glue • Cocktail sticks

Finished size: 30 cm (12 in) approx.

This galleon always looks splendid in all-white paper sculpture sailing on a deep blue background. An A2 (16¹/2 x 23³/8 in) coloured sheet is quite big enough to hold the whole image, including paper waves, and can always be trimmed down to size, if necessary, when the whole work is complete. I have designed this ship to fit easily into 'A' sizes of paper and the proportions of the hull, masts and sails reflect this restraint. Once you understand the basic principles of construction, altering these to make a more authentic model, such as Drake's 'Golden Hind' will present few problems.

PREPARATORY WORK

Fold and cut a sheet of A4 (8¹/4 x 11³/4 in) white paper in half Houses way round (landscape). Trace down the hull of the galleon, once you have enlarged the pattern accompanying this project on a photocopier, so it fits into one half of

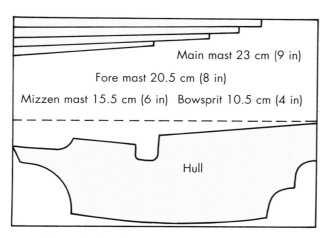

Main mast 23 cm (9 in)

Fore mast 20.5 cm (8 in)

Mizzen mast 15.5 cm (6 in)   Bowsprit 10.5 cm (4 in)

Hull

A4 (8¼ x 11¾ in) paper folded Houses way round (landscape) for hull and masts

Position your galleon's hull on the A2 (16½ x 23⅜ in) coloured paper, leaving enough room for a stormy sea at the bottom and space at the left hand side for the bowsprit. Mark the position of the tab with a pencil and then stick it into place. Lifting the hull carefully, apply a line of glue down the centre of each spacing cylinder and lower these into place, one at a time. Finally, fasten the pointed end of the bows to the background with a spot of PVA. These five gluing points should keep the whole hull secure and in place. If you design your own ship you may need to use different supports and spacers.

the paper. Cut this out carefully then cut three masts and a bowsprit from the other half. I like to taper these from 1 cm (½ in) at their base to 8 mm (5/16 in) at the top end. Fold and cut up a piece of A4 (8¼ x 11¾ in) paper for the sails and additional details as indicated in the diagrams.

HULL

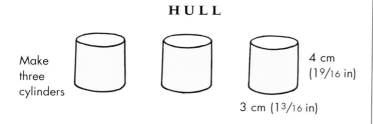

Make three cylinders

4 cm (19/16 in)

3 cm (13/16 in)

Make three cylinders 3 cm (1 in) in diameter by 4 cm (19/16 in) deep. These will space the hull away from the background and are fastened in place where shown. Take one of the smallest rectangles you cut for the sails and fold two tabs, 1 cm (½ in) wide, one at each end. Glue the tabbed rectangle inside the top of the stern or aft-castle. Once these supports and spacers are dry, turn the hull over and fasten it to an A2 (16½ x 23⅜ in) coloured background.

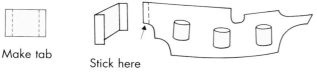

Make tab

Stick here

Glue cylinders on back of hull

MASTS

The masts and bowsprit are glued directly to the background, the three masts overlapping the edge of the hull at the back by about 1 cm (½ in). They can be stuck down flat or, for added interest, scored down the centre and creased to create a three-dimensional quality. In the latter case PVA needs to be applied carefully to the edges of the scored masts here and there. Treat the bowsprit in an identical manner to your masts, leaving a tiny gap of background colour showing between it and the end of the bows it rests on. Our mainmast goes in the centre of the hull and the foremast and mizzen about 8 cm (3³/16 in) away in each direction.

Score mast

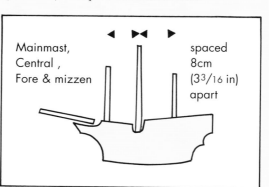

Mainmast, Central, Fore & mizzen

spaced 8cm (3³/16 in) apart

Stick masts and bowsprit to background; the masts overlap hull 1cm (½ in)

SAILS

Divide and cut an A4 (8¹/4 x 11³/4 in) piece of paper for the sails as shown in the diagram. I usually cut the concave base and side of the sails first and then trim the convex side to match the opposite curve. A triangular sail only needs the two edges at right angles to each other to be shaped. To curl them imagine each 'square' sail attached to a spar, put it on the table houses way round (landscape) and curve gently over the table's edge. The triangular sail needs to be curved at right angles to its straight edge. Once this shaping is complete turn all the sails over and glue a small cylinder on to the reverse side of each one. When the glue is dry, squash the end of the cylinder facing the convex edge of each sail to flatten it.

A4 (8¹/4 x 11³/4 in) cut as above for sails

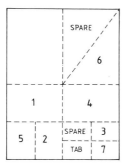

1-5

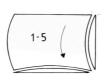

Cut sails like this

6

Squash cylinder here

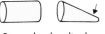
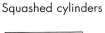

Squashed cylinders

Support sail with cylinder

Apply PVA to each sail cylinder in turn and glue down the sails in the number order shown, starting with the main mast. Position the sails dry first and be patient while the glue on each cylinder sets. Sail 7, the smallest, goes under the bowsprit. Allow all the sails to overlap naturally, remembering that the wind is blowing the vessel forwards.

DETAILS

Once the ship is complete in its basics you may add whatever details you wish. If you have tackled a number of other projects in the book this will be a relatively easy task.

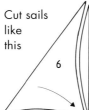

Flags

Here are some suggestions: cotton thread for rigging, a choppy sea, anchor and chain, crow's nest, life boats, wheel, wheelhouse, rudder and figurehead, flags, cannon and windows in the captain's cabin at the stern of your ship. If you are very nifty with scissors you might even be able to cut out a few sailors to crew your galleon.

HUMAN HEADS

EQUIPMENT & MATERIALS

A2 (16¹/₂ x 23³/₈ in) white paper (rough)
Small craft knife • Cutting mat
Scissors • 30 cm (1 ft) Plastic rule
A2 (16¹/₂ x 23³/₈ in) white paper
PVA glue • Cocktail sticks
A3 (11³/₄ x 16¹/₂ in) white paper
Pencil • Soft eraser

Finished size: approx. life size

When you start making heads it's best to allow the sculpture to dictate the outcome of the features rather than try to force this. Later, when you are proficient at all the processes involved, try a portrait head of yourself – it's a fascinating challenge.

As with all the work in this book I will be suggesting the simplest methods of making the features – many other possibilities are explored in the next project ISNOSMOWF.

Follow the diagrams accompanying the text instructions – they will illuminate the text and what is hard to explain in words will be more easily grasped from the pictures.

TO MAKE THE FACE

Fold a sheet of scrap A2 (16¹/₂ x 23³/₈ in) paper in half Houses way round (landscape) and cut it in two. Fold one sheet Flats way round (portrait) and draw your face pattern on to this. Cut out the pattern from the folded paper. Open the pattern out and check that the chin is rounded and slim enough.

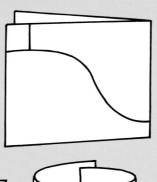

Trim where necessary, especially if it's pointed, as sometimes happens. At the top of the head-pattern, measure along the straight edge 25 cm (10¹/₂ in) from the fold, and cut off the excess. Open up the pattern and draw round it on to a good sheet of A2 (16¹/₂ x 23³/₈ in) white paper.

Cut out the face and join it at the back, gluing and overlapping by 1 cm (¹/₂ in). Put the head on one side while the glue dries.

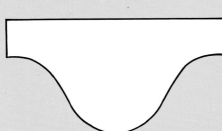
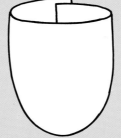

Cut out the head and glue at the back with a 1cm (¹/₂ in) overlap

NECK

Make a neck from an A3 (11³/₄ x 16¹/₂ in) sheet by curling it Flats way round (portrait) over the edge of a table. Judge how wide the neck should be by placing the roll inside the head; mark a 1 cm (¹/₂ in) overlap and cut off the excess before making the cylinder.

Once you stand up the head and the neck you may find the face sags slightly. Make a small cylinder and glue this in the space between neck and face, inside the head, and the face will be supported correctly.

To complete the basic form cut four strips of paper 3 cm (1³/₁₆ in) wide and glue these inside to form the top of the head. Remember that the top of the head is quite flat and feel your own to get an idea of the shape before you glue the strips in place. Do not make them too domed.

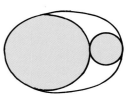

Make neck

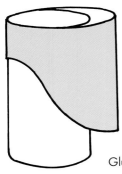

Glue the neck inside the head, exactly level with the top, making sure that the joints of both are in line. This is important for a neat finish.

Glue neck into head

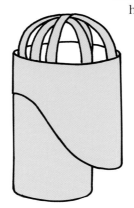

Glue four strips into the top of the head

EYES

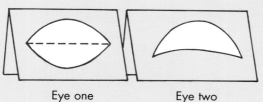

Eye one   Eye two

Cut simple eye-shapes from a fold of paper, scoring and creasing lengthwise – younger children can fold them – and add pupils before you glue them in place. The diagrams show three sorts: a circle, a circle with a 'V' cut out and a ring made from a thin strip of paper.

Open the eyes until they are at a slight angle and fasten the pupils in place with a dab of glue top and bottom, before gluing the eyes into position halfway down the head and an eye's distance apart.

Apply glue to the fold at the back of each eye. Lay the face down while you attach the eyes and the rest of the features, and leave until the glue is dry. With both eyes and mouth, ensure that only the fold is glued to the face, and that the sides are free to cast a slight shadow above and below these features. Eyes can also be made by cutting two wide moon shapes (see diagrams), curving these and gluing the pupils underneath. This is achieved by means of a small tab attached to the round pupil or by including the tab as part of this piece. Bend over the tab gently before you stick it underneath the eyelid. Put PVA along the edges of the eyelids to hold them in place. A thinner lower lid can be added in the same way.

Different pupil shapes

Pupil one

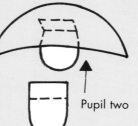

Pupil two

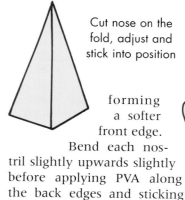

NOSE

A very basic nose can be cut from a fold of paper (the edge of the nose formed by this fold), making two straight cuts to form a triangle. You can soften this rather sharp image by using the shape as a pattern for a rounder version. Open the original, draw round it, round off the nostrils, and the bridge and tip of the nose with a pencil, and cut out the adjusted shape. With all marks inside, bend the nose lengthwise round a pencil

Cut nose on the fold, adjust and stick into position

forming a softer front edge. Bend each nostril slightly upwards slightly before applying PVA along the back edges and sticking into position.

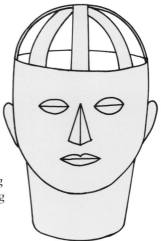

LIPS

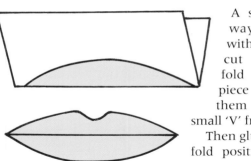

A straightforward way of dealing with the lips is to cut them on the fold from a small piece of paper, open them out and snip a small 'V' from the top lip. Then glue them on the fold positioned halfway between nose and chin.

Create more authentic lips by cutting a 'U' shape from a folded piece of paper, similar to a short duck's beak. Curl the two free, rounded ends in opposite directions round a pencil. Trim the top lip smaller and cut out its

'V'. Slide these lips through a slit made with a craft knife in the face between the nose and chin. Be very careful how you cut this slit. I use a small piece of board underneath to protect my fingers and also keep these as far away as I can from the blade. Apply a line of glue to the slit to keep the lips in place, or bend over the folded end once it is inside and secure.

EYEBROWS

Bend eyebrow like this

Eyebrows complete the features of the face and can add a great deal to the expression by their positioning, size and shape. Eyebrows can be smooth and arched, bushy and straight or any other way you desire. You can easily make them appear hairy by cutting small slits along their top edge. To attach them, bend each eyebrow so that it curves away from the brow, bend the ends straight again and glue them on with the two tabs you have created.

EARS

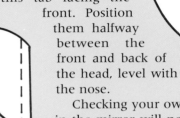

Very often hair hides some or all of the ears especially when it is long or very curly but I always include them anyway. Create ears by cutting out half a heart-shape on the fold of a piece of paper. This heart-shape should be the same length as the nose. Round the point with scissors, open out and cut along the fold. This will give you two simple ears which you can work on further if you wish.

To attach ears fold a thin tab along their straight edge and glue them in place with this tab facing the front. Position them halfway between the front and back of the head, level with the nose.

Checking your own face in the mirror will not only enable you to place the features on your paper sculpture head correctly but will often give ideas for different expressions, especially if you make faces at yourself and see how this subtly alters the positions of eyebrows, eyes, nose and mouth.

Using a strip of paper and marking off the sizes of parts of the face on its edge is an easy way to keep a portrait or self-portrait accurate.

If eyebrows are raised this looks like a greeting, furrowed together in the centre of the forehead gives an angry expression, while positioned out to the sides they give a sad look.

Think about their different expressions before you fasten them on, trying them in several places. Whatever you do, avoid sticking them flat on to the face because they will lose all their impact in this way.

HAIR

Hair, including moustaches and beards where appropriate, is the last addition to our human head and, like eyebrows, the style, length, curl or straightness of the hair will add a great deal of character to your sculpture. You will all know how much changes to your own hair can make a difference to how you look. Hair is added to the head as tiles are to a roof, starting at the bottom of the hairline and working towards the crown of the head. Strips of paper for the hair are best cut and glued on in twos or threes, joined at the top. Cut strips in a consistent width. Fine strips will look and curl very differently to wide ones. You will have to decide on the length and style of the hair, and it may be useful to try a few different approaches before gluing any strips in place.

CURLS

For curly hair use scissors or pencil to curl a part, or the whole, of a strip. Subtle bending will give a wavy alternative. Long hair may be bent gently, with curls at the end of the length, as though it has been put in rollers. Curls may face out from the head or into the cheek, or nape of the neck.

CRIMPED

Crimped hair is created by fan-folding each set of strips after they have been cut. An untidy version can be easily achieved by holding the joined end of the locks and completely crumpling up the strips in the other hand. Tease these apart to give a very fashionable 'scruffy' look.

SHORT HAIR

Short stubbly hair is easy to create but takes a lot of patience both in the cutting and application to the head. But, done well, it can look really good, and the length can be trimmed just like real hair, once all the pieces are securely fastened to the head of the sculpture.

Short, soft styles for both men and women can be made by using leaf shapes for each lock of hair, again cutting the textural strips into these from one pointed end and side, leaving the other point for fixing to the head. These leaf-shaped locks are

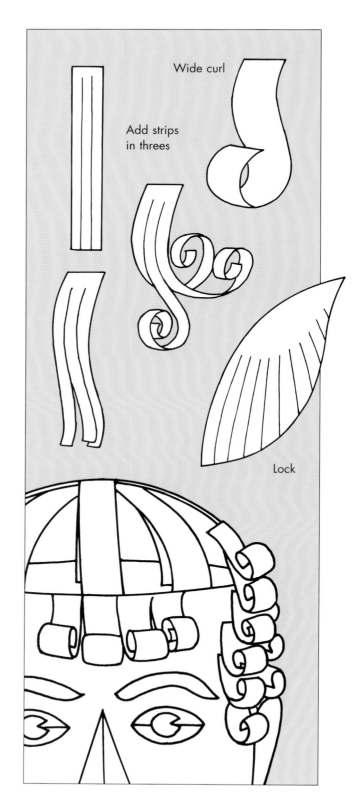

Wide curl

Add strips in threes

Lock

applied in the same way as you
would the strips, starting at the
nape of the neck, above the
ears and from the forehead,
overlapping as you go and
working towards the
crown of the head. I
usually mark the crown
with a scrap of masking
tape, or paper which
can be removed later,
because it is all too
easy, when you are
absorbed in the work,
to forget that the hair
comes together at the
back of the head rather than
the top.

HATS

If you intend to put a hat on your
paper sculpture portrait, do this
before adding the hair. All kinds
of hats and caps are possible but
beware of bowlers because of
the real difficulty in constructing a smooth dome.

Beards, moustaches, glasses,
eyelashes, earrings and necklaces
are a few of the extras you may
wish to consider adding to your
sculpture. Keep the Five Basic
Techniques in mind as you experiment with the paper and you will be
able to add convincing details to complete the head. Use the minimum of
glue for all small pieces as over-zealous
applications can give problems with
dirty glue-marks spoiling an otherwise
excellent piece of work.

I enjoy making faces more than any other
subject, because different expressions have
always fascinated me and I find it a real
challenge to try and create a particular
'look' in paper: I hope you will too!

PROJECT 16

ISNOSMOWF

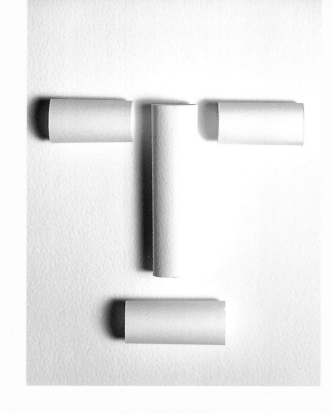

I hope you were curious enough to wonder what on earth this project was about when you read the list of contents. It's really about EYES, NOSES, MOUTHS, EARS, HAIR and so on, but this seemed too much for a title! Some years ago I had made an exhibition piece with all twenty four of these faces and used the same title, so I thought it appropriate to repeat here.

Eyes, nose and mouth are the only features given in the faces, but it will only take a little thought to add matching eyebrows, ears and hair. In most cases, in fact, there will be a number of different solutions and you may be able to choose the most suitable for creating a particular expression, or to portray different facial features, or to set the face firmly in a century or fashionable era. Women and children are often sculpted with softer, smoother faces than men due to the differences in bone structure and musculature, so this will need consideration too.

At the end of the project you will find further suggestions for a variety of eyebrows, ears, hair, moustaches and beards. This will enable you to create a wide range of different faces, each with a unique character.

There are twenty four different faces described here to give you an insight into the tremendous range of features you can create from paper. Varying the proportions of the eyes, nose and mouth will often completely alter the expression of a face.

FACE 1

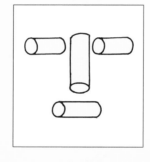

This face made with four cylinders of equal width, can be changed by varying the length of the cylinders, changing their spacing, having cylinders of different widths and, possibly, cutting the ends off at an angle rather than having them straight.

FACE 2

Eyes and mouth are created from three strips scored, creased and glued so that the sides project toward you. The nose is the same shape reversed with its edges stuck to the paper. I like to make the nose narrower at its bridge and wider at its end and also taper the sides in a similar manner.

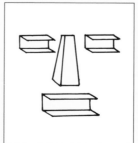

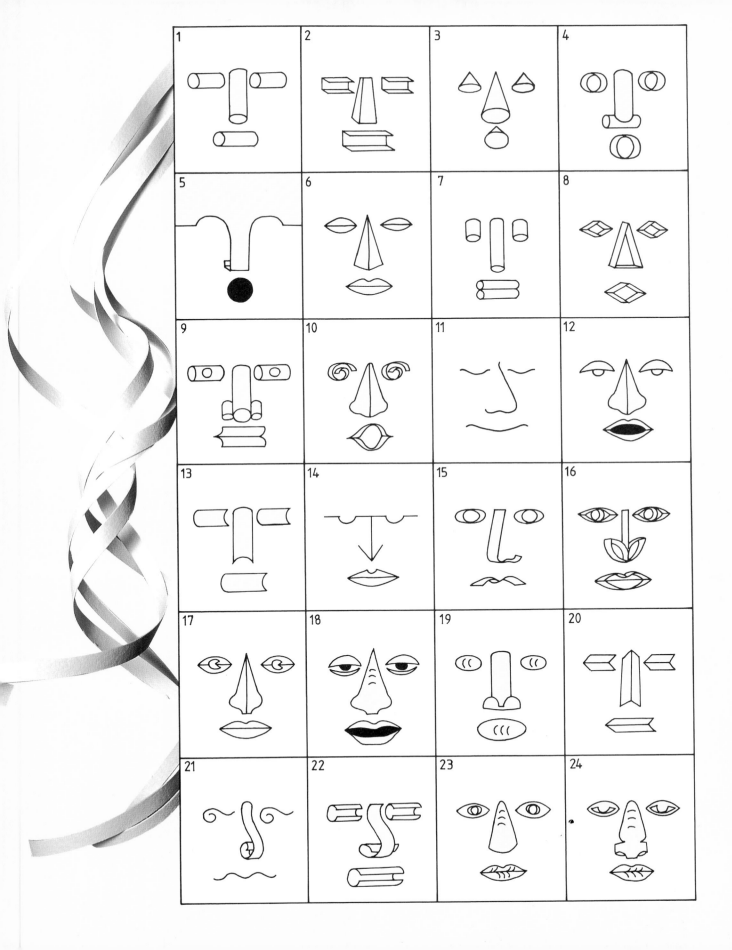

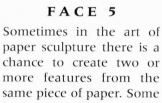

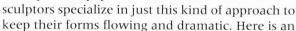

FACE 3

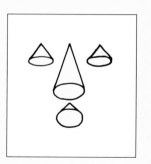

Cones are always awkward to make because of the tapered overlap which disappears to nothing at the point. Large cones can be formed from a quarter circle but these four small ones are better made from larger segments, up to a whole circle with a slit, if need be. Note that they are of slightly different proportions with the mouth cone being the shallowest. Keep your joins neat and glue-free on the inside because they will be seen when the cones are stuck down in position.

FACE 4

This face again uses cylinders, but this time eyes and mouth are formed by gluing them on edge. Two cylinders at right angles make the nose. You could shape the end of the one which forms the long axis of the nose for a snug fit. All the cylinders can be squashed slightly to make them elliptical and alter the expression of the face, or well-flattened to change it even more.

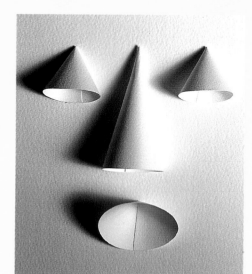

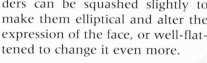

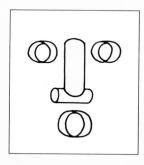

FACE 5

Sometimes in the art of paper sculpture there is a chance to create two or more features from the same piece of paper. Some sculptors specialize in just this kind of approach to keep their forms flowing and dramatic. Here is an example in which the eyebrows and the nose are cut from a single piece of paper. Note that the nose strip must be long enough to be bent over twice to accommodate the depth of the nose and a tab for attaching it to the face. A round or oval mouth is cut out of the piece it is joined to.

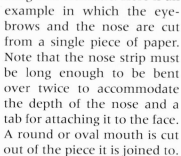

FACE 6

If you have made a Father Christmas or human face you will know that this is the basic face I advocated. Both eyes and mouth are similar leaf-shapes, folded or scored, and creased from corner to corner. The top lip is trimmed to its special shape and a triangular nose cut on the fold of a piece of paper added to complete the set. When positioning the parts of the face, I invariably place the eyes first then add the nose and finally the mouth but, if you do a dry run, the features could go on in any order and be re-positioned until you are satisfied with the result; then one piece at a time can be lifted and glued back into its place.

FACE 7

Another variation with cylinders is to turn the two eye-rolls facing downwards and make two smaller ones for the lips. The nose is the same as the one in FACE 1.

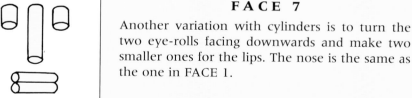

FACE 8

Three diamonds and a triangle create a very different look here. These are made from four strips of identical width, folded and joined with an integral tab. PVA along the edges will set them into place but be sure that the positioning is correct to avoid spreading the glue around. A couple of faint pencil marks or dots will help with accurate placing.

FACE 9

This time eyes and nose are cylindrical but the mouth is made differently. Fold a rectangle of paper at least twice as long as its width and curl the two open ends outwards. You may like to roll the open ends opposite ways using a round pencil as a former as I prefer to do. Once rolled, the lips are passed through a slit in the face and fastened at the back with glue or a tab. Cut out the pupils from the centre of the rectangles for the eye cylinders before you curl and glue them.

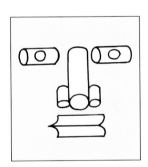

FACE 10

Strips are very versatile and can provide all kinds of shapes for the facial features like these spiral eyes, which are cartoon-like in character. Form the mouth from a curled strip joined to make a circle and then pinched at both sides. Hold these two pinched points and push them gently inwards to coax the top and bottom parts of the strip back into its circular shape. Make the nose from a fourth strip, spiralled at one end like a very curly question mark.

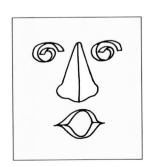

FACE 11

Cutting directly into the paper is an interesting technique which requires a confident approach or a reversed drawing on the back of the paper. This face is cut with a small, sharp craft knife and then each cut is lifted from the front or pushed out from the back, very gently with the fingers, to give the eyes, nose and mouth some sculptural form. I have, on occasions, drawn my image on thin layout or tracing paper and laid this on top of my sculpture paper, and cut through both together. You must use a very sharp blade or one sheet of paper may catch and tear, or the cut may be rough or ragged. If you use disposable blades in a scalpel handle, change to a new one when cutting through two layers. It is quite difficult to give paper faces a smiling mouth, especially one with a slight grin, but this is one of the ways of achieving it.

FACE 13

Another simple but effective face, consisting of four curved strips. These are curved across their width round a former such as a piece of dowelling or a cardboard roll. Alternatively, four pieces could be cut off a well curled rectangle and then trimmed to length. Both 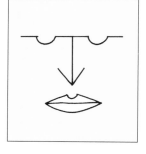 the eyes and the mouth are set in position with their concave side upwards and the nose, glued down by its edges, is convex. This arrangement gives a subtlety to the light and shade in white paper and could also be reversed with equal effectiveness.

FACE 12

A variation on the basic face, the eyes are made differently here, the top eyelids being cut from a fold of paper. Both pupils are made from short strips rounded at one end, with its opposite square end bent to form a tab. Use this to attach the pupils inside the eyelids once these have been gently curved with scissors. Nostrils are added to the usual triangular nose as it is cut out on the fold and these are bent slightly upwards. The nose is then stuck on, by gluing its straight edges.

This open mouth is more awkward to cut out because you must ensure the two lips remain joined together. Cut a shallow half-moon shape from a doubled over piece of paper then snip out the "V" in the top lip before applying glue to the inside edges of the lips to secure them in place. Once the glue is thoroughly dry you may wish to cut out the space between the lips, as I have in the diagram above.

FACE 14

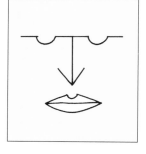

Strips again form the basis of these strange features and are, as usual, fixed on edge. This process is easier when the paper is of a reasonable weight. Create the pupils of the eyes by folding the paper at either side of the round section and then use scissors or a former to curve the paper between these two folds. Score-lines can be used instead of folds and will provide a crisper finish. A smaller curve is needed in the centre of the top lip to echo the pupils or you may prefer to fold a 'V' instead.

FACE 15

Elliptical eyes, created by carefully squashing two circles made with strips, matched with a nose and mouth bent carefully to the shape of a wobbly 'L' and a bow give a very different character to this face. A cocktail stick is perfect for applying glue to all these edges but do remember to change it as soon as the end becomes gummed up with the adhesive.

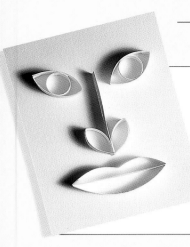

FACE 16

Strip construction gives the effect of quilling in the shapes of eyes, nose and mouth here. I prefer to make all the parts separately and glue them together but, with a little ingenuity, you could certainly form the nose and mouth from single strips. Small, integral tabs are used to join the lengths once they have been shaped. Add the pupils and the centre line for the lips after the outside leaf-shapes are completed.

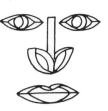

FACE 17

Several of the faces given here are variations on a basic theme. This one is very similar to FACE 6 but notched pupils have been added to the eyes and the nose has two side flaps and an extension to its end. This extension is a short strip which curls under to form two nostril spaces and, at its end, provides a tab which is glued to the face.

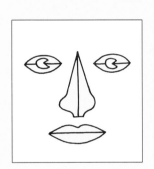

FACE 18

These eyes are made as described for FACE 12 but the pupils are cut away and have additional lower lids, which need curving slightly before gluing in place. This nose, although similar to the one on the previous face, does not have a fold running down its length. The middle section, from the bridge to tip, is rolled round a pencil (not a hexagonal one), or thin dowel to give a wider, softer contour to the nose.

Two separate lips are cut and curved, then fastened to the face. This allows a variety of expressions not present in the more geometric lip forms. If the lips are parted, as these are, cut out the space between with a very sharp scalpel when all glue is thoroughly dry. A small, curved scrap of paper can be fixed behind the mouth if the cut out space appears too darkly shadowed.

FACE 19

Three elliptical pieces of paper are slightly curved across their width for eyes and mouth, which are stuck down so that the concave side is towards you. This curvature creates a shadow both behind and within the form, giving them a sculptural quality. This effect can be intensified by spacing any of the facial parts further from their background, thus increasing the shadow. Two oval flaps are cut and bent outwards at the end of the cylindrical nose for nostrils. Small, sharp scissors are the best tools for snipping these out or try the deft use of a craft knife. Watch your fingers with the latter though, as red and white paper sculpture should be deliberate rather than accidental! A faint pencil mark will help guide you while cutting and keep both sides even. Remove the graphite by dabbing it away with a putty rubber before you manipulate the flaps.

FACE 20

'V'-shaped strips folded, or scored and creased, are used for all these facial pieces. Eyes are glued on the fold, facing upwards, so that both edges are at 45° to the face. Mountain-fold the nose and glue it on by its edges. Lips are two fan-folds fastened on by their creases. If you scored the nose and eyes, repeat this process with the mouth.

FACE 24

In the last face in this series the usual leaf shapes for the eyes are folded then flattened before the whites of the eyes are cut away with a scalpel, leaving the pupils attached to the top lids. Re-fold before gluing them down. A more elaborate version of the nose we used for FACE 18 is employed here, the end having three strips instead of one. Nostrils are formed by extending the flaps into short strips in an identical way to the end of the nose. A short cut is made above each nostril strip so that the triangular sides of the nose can be bent to touch the face. Round off the bridge of the nose then roll up the three strips, trimming their lengths if necessary. Make sure the sides and strips are correctly positioned before you glue the nose down.

Lips are a folded rectangle of paper rounded at its open end, and both flaps curled outwards with scissors or bent over a round pencil. Trim the top lip to a shallower curve, remembering to indent its centre, then slide the folded end through a slit cut below the nose. Secure the lips by folding them over at the back and sticking the spare paper down. Spread glue along the slit in the face or fasten with a small tab again at the back of the work.

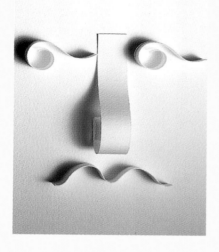

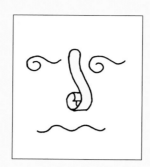

FACE 21

Quite a number of these images are very graphic, almost like line drawings of the face in the fine edges of the strips. Spirals with curved ends for the eyes and nose and a wavy mouth give an enigmatic look here. Each strip needs to be fully formed before it is glued into place, or the spring in the paper will pull it out of position.

FACE 22

Form the cylinders for eyes and mouth but, instead of overlapping them and so on, leave them unjoined and glue in place with the opening showing at the front. The nose is a strip which widens at one end, with this wide part curled to give nostrils.

FACE 23

This is a variation of our basic model with leaf-shaped eyes and mouth cut on the fold and a simple nose made from a triangle of paper with its centre bent over a round pencil. This time the pupils are made from thin strips formed into circles. Curve the lips round the pencil as well before you stick them down by their fold.

FACIAL EXPRESSION

We all watch faces and facial expressions more than any other part of the human body because each fleeting change is a subtle language by which we learn to read other people's moods and re-actions. Children are much better at assimilating this unspoken information.

To produce convincing paper sculpture faces you will need to re-learn this skill. I carry a small sketchbook and quickly scribble down actual faces whenever I can, and also doodle different heads from my imagination. A third way is to play with paper, arranging and re-arranging basic forms which represent eyes, nose and mouth, with the possibility of changing each one using our familiar five – cut, fold, curl, bend and score.

FINISHING TOUCHES

Grow a moustache, change your hairstyle, pluck your eyebrows and your friends and family may well look at you differently, so the rest of this project is devoted to ways you can treat the hair, ears, eyebrows, beards and moustaches of your subjects.

HAIR

A crucial part of creating hair is in the width of the strips cut into the paper. As natural hair differs in texture, not only from person to person, but racially too, you will need to experiment by cutting locks of hair from fine to broad – before you style them with the following techniques:

SHAPING

It is rare to see absolutely straight hair and a slight bend can be made by stroking the strips, letting them pass between thumb and fingers and, at the same time, turning your hand over enough to give the desired curvature. Long hair often has curly ends so just deal with this portion of the strips. My own preference is to add curly ends once the locks have been glued on to the head and shaped.

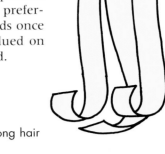

Long hair

CURLS

Tight curls are made using scissors or by rolling strips tightly round a pencil or dowel of the appropriate diameter.

Permed hair will use wider strips than the naturally curly variety. Wind the paper down a round pencil at 45° to form ringlets. Angling your scissors at 45° as you curl will also work, though this is harder to control and gives a more modern casual look to the hair, especially with fine strips.

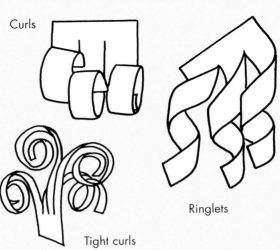

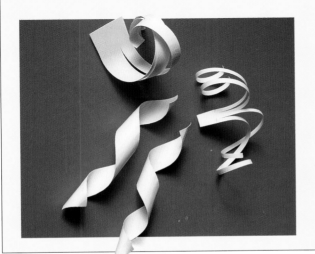

Curls

Tight curls

Ringlets

WAVES & CRIMPS

Wavy locks are easy to create if you keep to the rule of applying them in units of three or four strips at a time. Loosely fold these over, holding them with your fingers between the folds to avoid creasing, to achieve a wonderfully wavy finished effect.

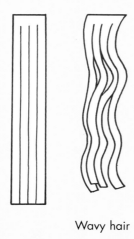

Wavy hair

Crease all the folds tightly and the same technique will give a crimped finish. Hold the joined end of the strips and scrunch the rest up in your hand as if you were screwing the piece up to throw it away and you will have a very free punk coiffure. Use this style loosely crumpled or teased apart for a really wild style.

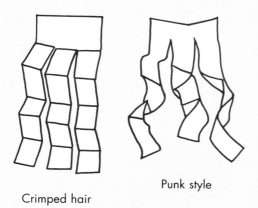

Crimped hair

Punk style

SHORT STYLES

Short, stubbly crew-cut styles are easy to snip out, but need patience to apply because you will need many pieces to cover the whole head, although the finished effect is well worth the effort as the textural effect is tremendous.

All hair styles need attaching to the hairline, at the forehead, above the ears and nape of the neck first, working upwards towards the crown of the head.

This applies particularly to short hair when it may be difficult to glue one piece underneath another successfully if a gap is left accidentally .

LOCKS

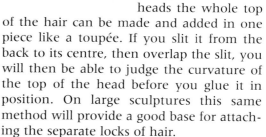

Another way of dealing with the hair is to divide it into locks and cut strips into these from one side or all round. Locks can be any shape, as long as the end which is to be attached to the head is tapered to a point. For small heads the whole top

Lock of hair

of the hair can be made and added in one piece like a toupée. If you slit it from the back to its centre, then overlap the slit, you will then be able to judge the curvature of the top of the head before you glue it in position. On large sculptures this same method will provide a good base for attaching the separate locks of hair.

FRINGES

Make fringes to match your locks by cutting out a suitable circular segment and making your slits from the circumference towards the centre. A few guidelines in pencil on the reverse will help you achieve the correct taper and length for these.

Fringe pattern

LONG STYLES

Usually each section of strips is glued on to hang downwards but, when long hair is tied up into a pony tail, wound into a bun or pulled back tight from the forehead and plaited, the temptation is to fasten the strips on in the direction of the pull. In fact, strips need to be put on opposite to this direction and, when the glue is thoroughly dry, gently turned over, making a much more natural join at the hairline for a realistic effect.

Strips are attached to the hairline

Hair is pulled back over head

PLAITS

Plaits are made in the same way you would plait real hair except that each strip of paper needs to be turned right over to get it to cross the adjacent length. A bow will disguise the join between the plaited portion of the hair and the additional, finer strips making the free end.

PARTINGS

Partings are created by gluing the hair down to a supporting strip in the opposite direction to that in which it will finish. Once dry, the hair is gently bent back to its correct side and secured. Deal with one side at a time, while making partings, or you will have a confusion of paper to sort out.

Below: These two figures have fringes created using the method described on this page.

EARS

Simple ears, of the kind we made in the last project cut on a fold of paper, can be much improved by drawing the outline from life. Have someone pose for you for a couple of minutes while you sketch the correct shape of the ear, remembering to add extra for the folded tab at the front edge. I usually slit the face and slide in the tab, fastening it on the inside of the head, thereby achieving a neater join than sticking it on the outside. Ears can be worked on further by cutting in all or part of the inner shapes, then pushing these back slightly to give a three-dimensional effect. This effect can be further enhanced by gluing a thin strip of paper round the edge of the ear, finishing it with an extra lobe, which has been bent slightly and then glued on top of the original one.

EYELASHES

Women's portraits may also benefit by having fine lashes cut for the upper lid of the eye. These must be done subtly and finely cut unless a caricatured effect is intended, when it may be appropriate to add lower eyelashes too. Curl lashes gently round a cocktail stick for the best effect. Once they are relaxed in this way and fastened on, you can adjust the curvature with your fingers and trim the length with scissors to suit the face.

EYEBROWS

Eyebrows can almost create an expression on their own, whether sad, angry or raised high in surprise and greeting; so make the most of them and try and get the shape and texture right for the face you are creating. Women and children usually have smoother eyebrows, whereas men and old people of both sexes are generally more hirsute, and with coarser textured hair. The shape, length and depth of each eyebrow and the angle, number and size of the small cuts you make to represent their texture will matter as much as the positions in which they are placed on the face. With curly eyebrows, allow plenty of width as curling will reduce this substantially.

Look at your own brows to ascertain the direction of cutting. This is mostly vertical, at the wide end near the bridge of the nose, ranging through to horizontal as the eyebrow comes round the face. Bend each one before you stick it on and also create a small tab at each end to receive the glue, because only these ends are attached to the head.

I remember as a child, reading my favourite comics and being fascinated that the comic heroes Dan Dare and Superman both had dissimilar eyebrows. My family must have been really worried for a while as my face tried to make one stay up and the other down, one curved and its neighbour straight. Eyebrows are rarely the same and individual treatment of these features can be used to enliven a paper sculptor's portrait considerably. Under normal circumstances, however, this will not be necessary and they can be cut as a pair.

Bend and glue tabs at end of eyebrows

BEARDS

Beards vary greatly from face to face and may be straggly, bushy, curly, long and straight, neatly trimmed or casual, and so on, and once again you need to create a texture in the hair appropriate to your subject. Beards can be added all in one piece, as several overlapping sections or as individual tufts of one to three strips. It is best to build these pieces on from the back of the face forwards, and upwards to form the hairline if this is appropriate for your chosen style. Photographic or drawn reference from life cannot be bettered in understanding the way a beard fits on to the face and the direction of the hair-growth.

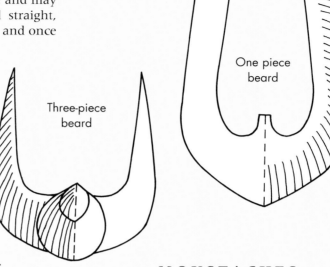

Three-piece beard

One piece beard

MOUSTACHES

This information is also relevant to moustaches which, in many men, form part of the beard structure and blend in with it. Where this is so I build the moustache in pieces, starting from the top lip and working downwards to join the beard. Another option is to cut the complete moustache from a folded rectangle of paper and hold this together while you cut in the hair strips. Once opened up, you can work on each side by curling and bending the individual hairs of the moustache. If necessary, additional tufts can be added to make each side of the moustache bushier.

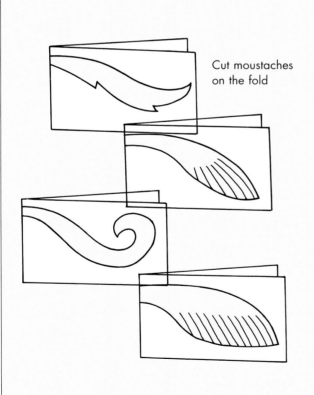

Cut moustaches on the fold

ADDING CHARACTER

Once the physical features are in place you can indulge yourself with all manner of fashion accessories and accoutrements such as hats, earrings and glasses to further enhance the character.

Follow flights of fancy, sculpt a self portrait, invent a geometric robot head or a political caricature; faces are fascinating to explore in paper.

TEMPLATES

PROJECT 1 –
FINGER PUPPET
Enlarge 50%

Large cylinder

Finger puppet neck

Small cylinder

Finger puppet head

PROJECT 2 – LANTERN AND LETTERBOX

Enlarge 85%

Cuboid Lantern & Letterbox

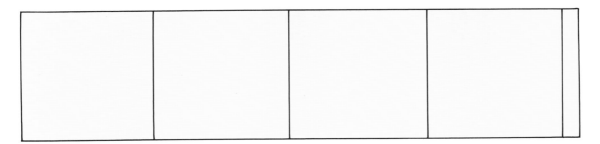

Cube

PROJECT 3 – LITTLE BIRD

Enlarge 40%

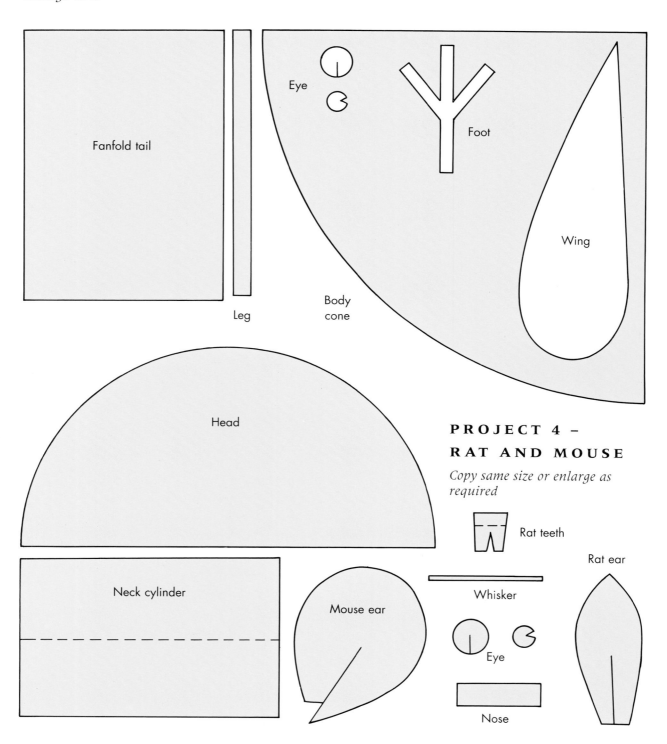

Fanfold tail

Leg

Body cone

Eye

Foot

Wing

Head

Neck cylinder

PROJECT 4 – RAT AND MOUSE

Copy same size or enlarge as required

Rat teeth

Whisker

Mouse ear

Eye

Nose

Rat ear

PROJECT 5 – RAFT

Enlarge 85%

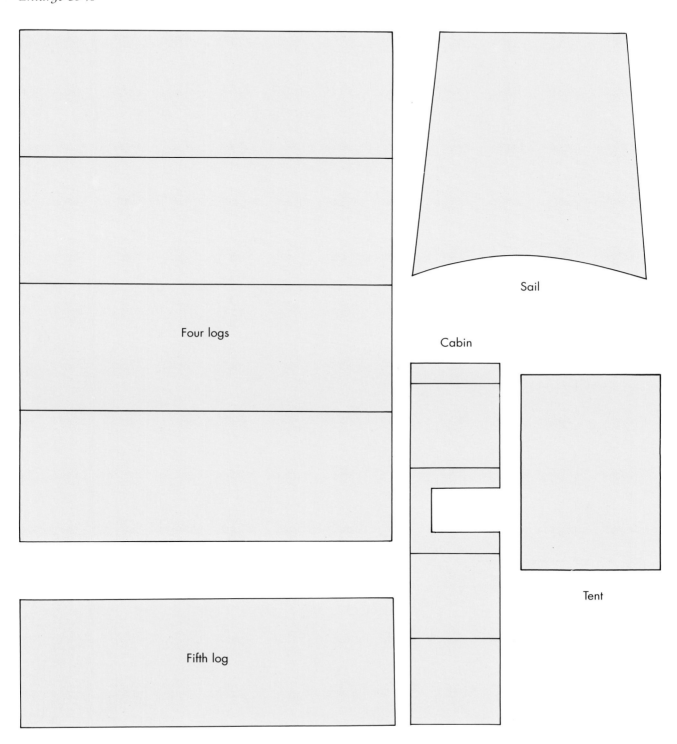

Sail

Cabin

Four logs

Tent

Fifth log

PROJECT 6 – FISH
Enlarge 108%

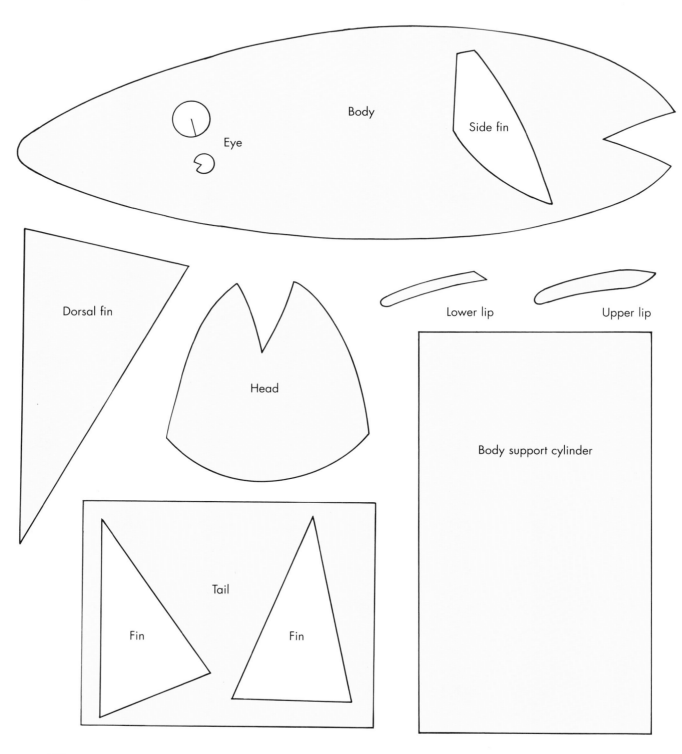

PROJECT 7 – OWL

Enlarge 85%

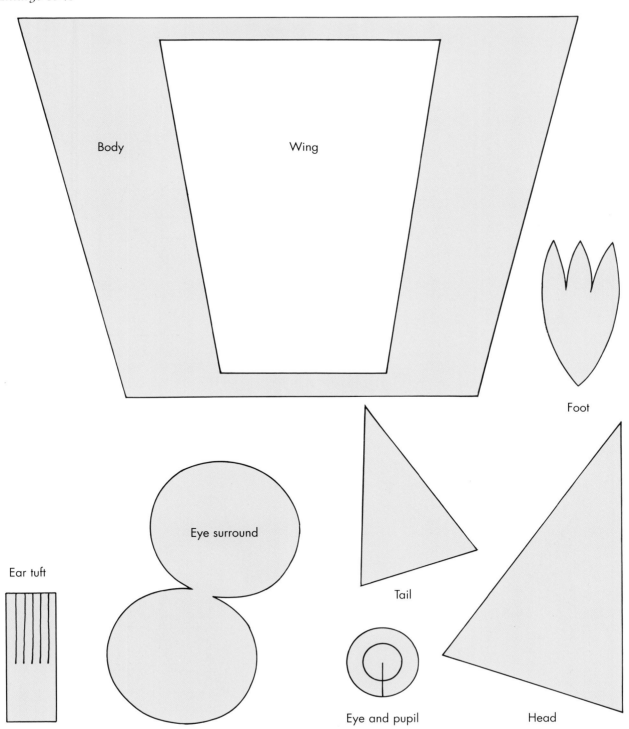

Body

Wing

Foot

Ear tuft

Eye surround

Tail

Eye and pupil

Head

PROJECT 9 – LEAVES

Copy same size or enlarge as required

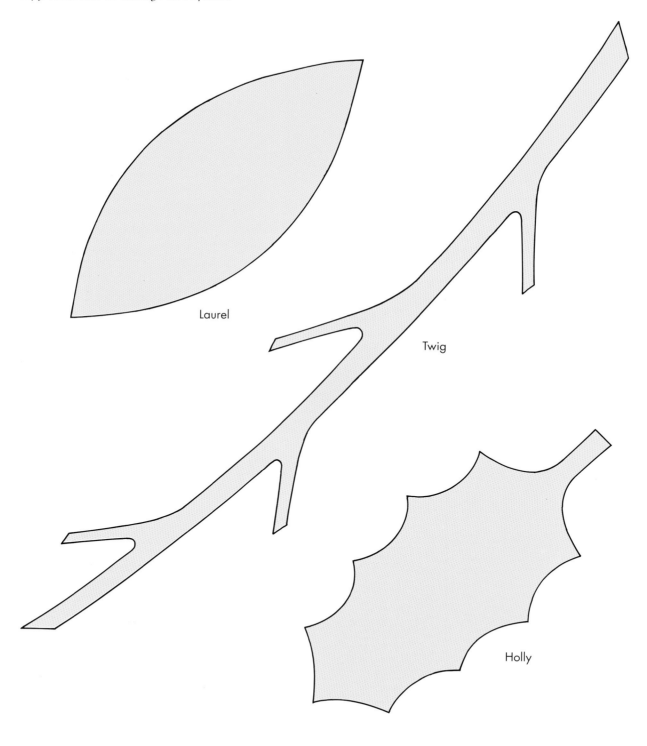

Laurel

Twig

Holly

PROJECT 10 – FLOWERS

Copy same size or enlarge as required

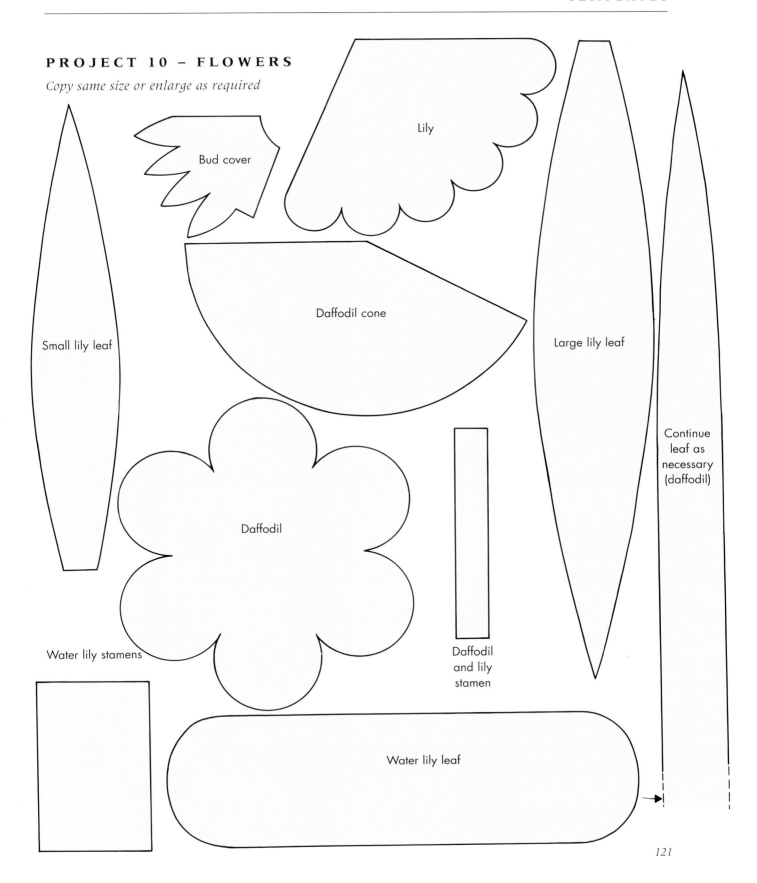

Bud cover

Lily

Small lily leaf

Daffodil cone

Large lily leaf

Continue leaf as necessary (daffodil)

Daffodil

Daffodil and lily stamen

Water lily stamens

Water lily leaf

PROJECT 11 – FIERY DRAGON'S HEAD
Enlarge 128%

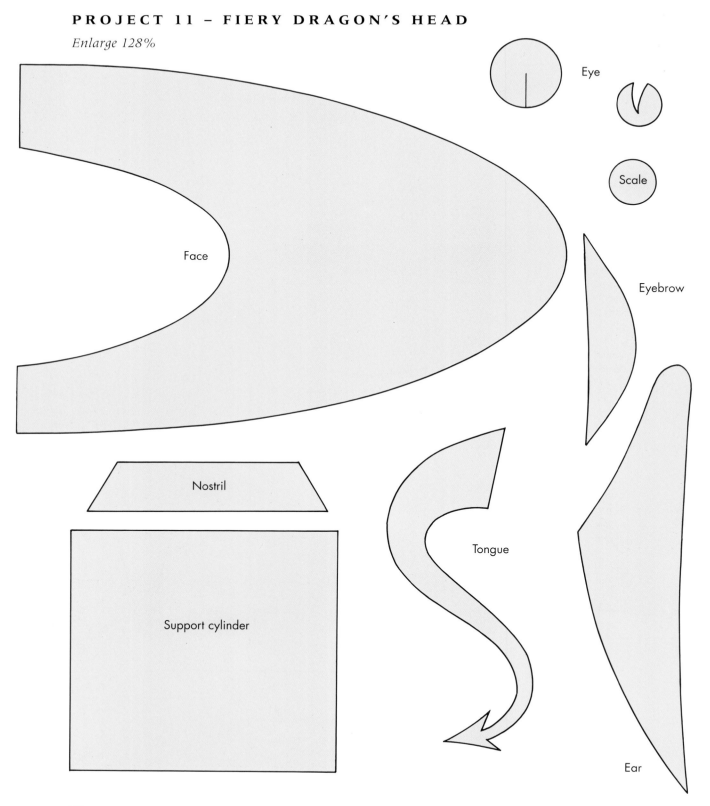

Eye

Scale

Face

Eyebrow

Nostril

Tongue

Ear

Support cylinder

PROJECT 12 – FATHER CHRISTMAS

Enlarge 108%

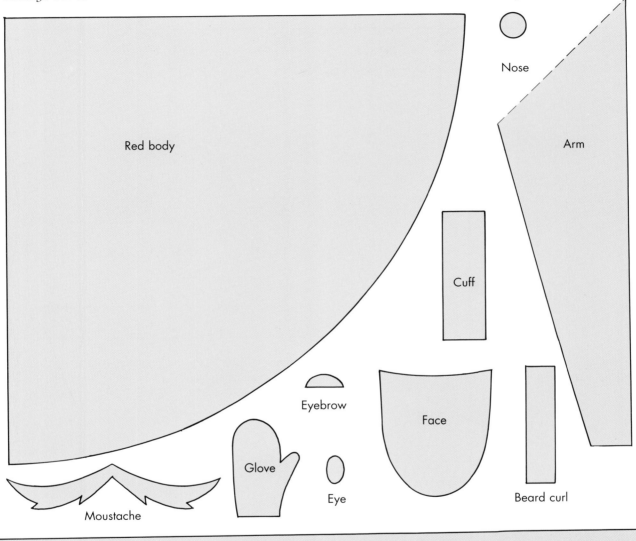

PROJECT 13 – ANGEL

Enlarge 110%

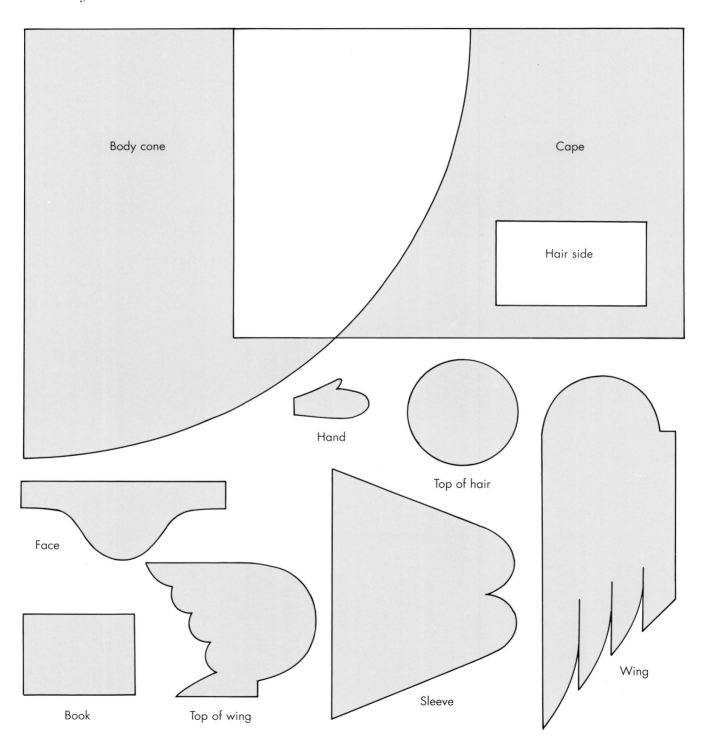

Body cone

Cape

Hair side

Hand

Top of hair

Face

Wing

Book

Top of wing

Sleeve

PROJECT 14 – GALLEON

Enlarge 79%

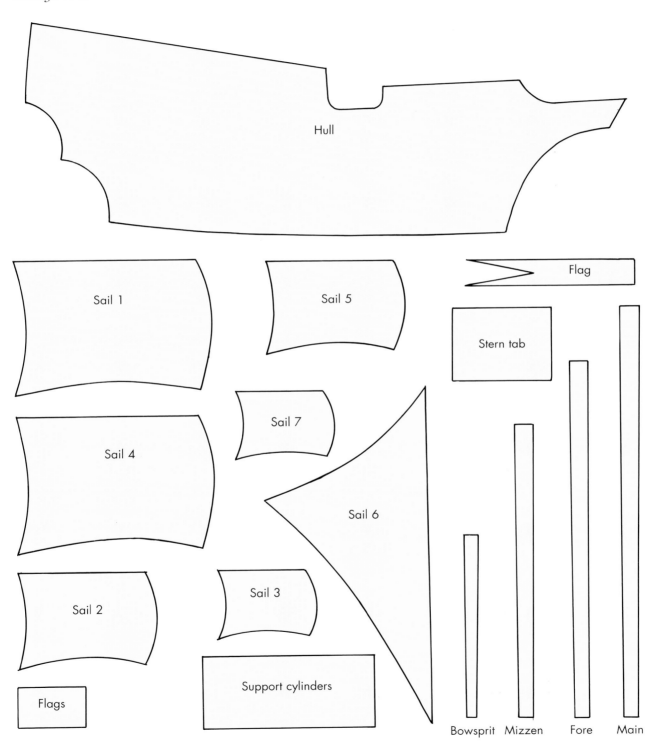

Hull

Sail 1

Sail 5

Flag

Stern tab

Sail 4

Sail 7

Sail 6

Sail 2

Sail 3

Support cylinders

Flags

Bowsprit   Mizzen   Fore   Main

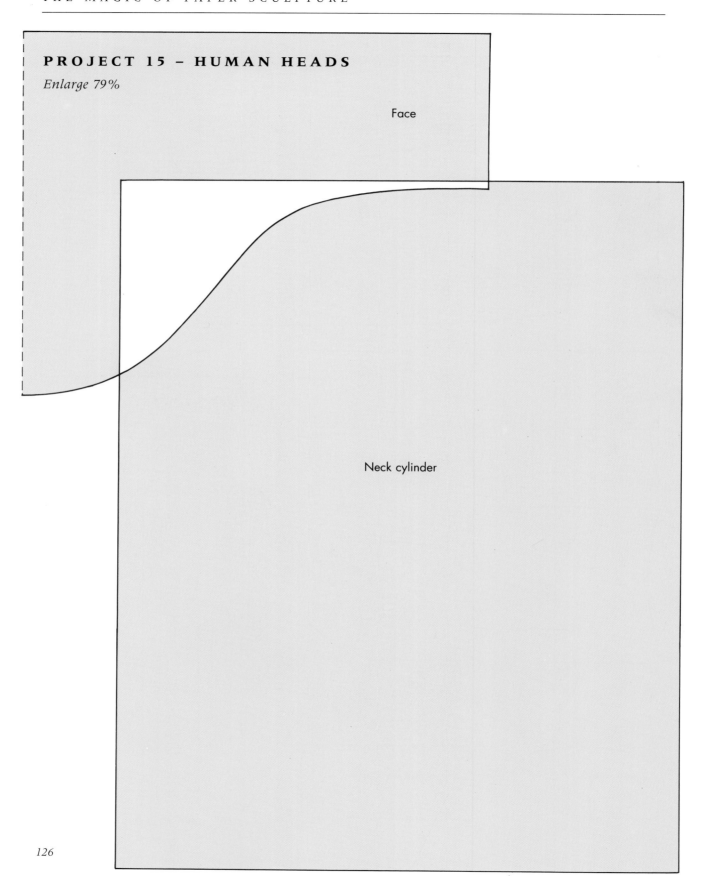

PROJECT 15 – HUMAN HEADS

Enlarge 79%

Face

Neck cylinder

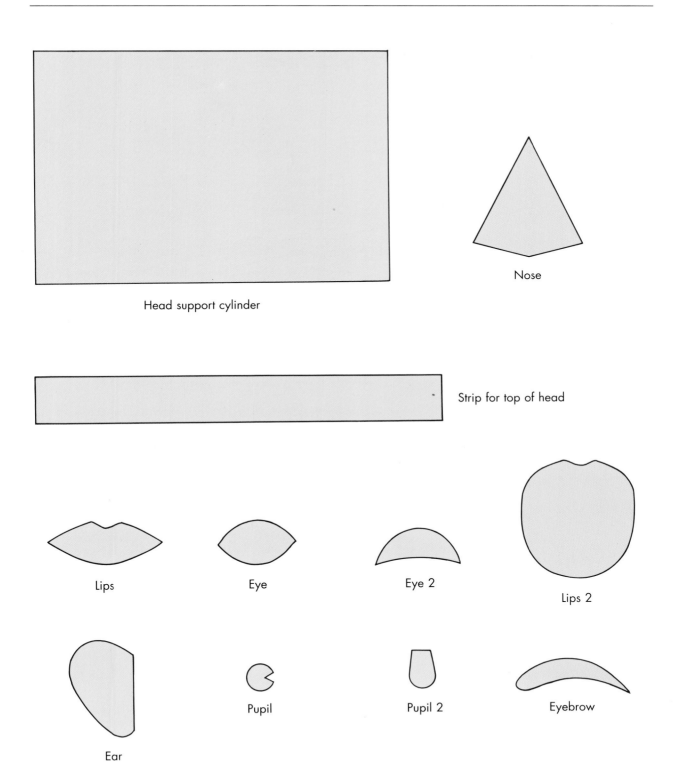

Head support cylinder

Nose

Strip for top of head

Lips

Eye

Eye 2

Lips 2

Ear

Pupil

Pupil 2

Eyebrow

INDEX